THE BEST OF
OUR WORLD

The WORLD of Professional Pet Sitting

Vol. 1 • 1994-1999

This book is dedicated to all of the pet sitters who have contributed to the pages of *The WORLD of Professional Pet Sitting* since 1994. From the beginning, I asked PSI members to provide their input and experience, to question and contribute—in short, to continue the very spirit of support and networking that PSI was founded on. And you have not let me down. From the original handful of professional pet sitters who constituted PSI's "founding" members to the more than 7,600 PSI members today, the sharing goes on. Thanks, to those of you who have contributed in the past, as well as those who will contribute in the future.

Patti J. Moran, PSI President

King, NC, May 2007

Published by
Pet Sitters International
201 East King Street
King, NC 27021

ISBN 978-0-9796488-0-9

This book has been published with the intention of providing factual information in regard to all subject matter. Every precaution to ensure accuracy has been taken in preparation of these materials; however, the publisher assumes no responsibility for errors or omissions; neither is any liability assumed for damages resulting from the use of any information found within these pages.

10 9 8 7 6 5 4 3 2

THE BEST OF OUR WORLD
Vol. 1 • 1994-1999

Contents

THE BEST OF
OUR WORLD
The WORLD of Professional Pet Sitting

Vol. 1 • 1994-1999

Welcome!

Welcome to *The WORLD of Professional Pet Sitting*. Since its introduction in 1994, *The WORLD* has been one of the most important benefits of membership in Pet Sitters International. From 1994 to 1999 PSI grew from a handful of members to more than 2,000 pet sitters in all 50 states, Canada and many other countries across the globe. During that time professional pet sitting was becoming a recognized and respected industry—and *The WORLD* was part of that process.

The WORLD provided the first forum (remember this was before the Internet made chat groups available) where pet sitters could learn, share ideas and business tips that helped many businesses become successful. Since much of what appeared in those early issues of *The WORLD* is still relevant to today's pet-sitting professional, we've decided to make this compilation of articles available. We think you'll find valuable information tucked away in every article.

So sit back, relax, and learn...but most of all enjoy

The Best of *Our* WORLD
The WORLD of Professional Pet Sitting

As pet sitting as an industry developed, grew and expanded, so did *The WORLD*. So let's begin with a quick timeline of the major changes we've seen over the years.

We're sure you'll see that at times *The WORLD* reflected improvements in the pet-sitting industry and at other times it *initiated* changes in the way pet sitters do business.

1994 *The WORLD of Professional Pet Sitting* began in May 1994 as an eight-page newsletter. The premier issue introduced many columns and concepts that are still around today, including "Bright Ideas," "Vets on Pets" and that familiar closing to all of Patti Moran's columns, "And now, read on."

Coordinator's Corner
by Patti J. Moran (August 1994)

The intent of this publication is to serve as an educational forum for our readers. With the variable nature of our business (No two pets, homes or clients are the same!), no one of us has all the answers when it comes to pet sitting. However, working together for the common good, we can seek answers and find solutions. And that's why your input is critical.

Sharing ideas, tips and opinions is what makes *The WORLD* so interesting—and PSI membership so beneficial! Sure, Bill Foster and I can espouse our views 'til the cows come home, but I guarantee you'll enjoy reading what pet sitters throughout the world have to say. Please let us hear from you!

And now, read on,
Patti Moran
PSI President

THE WORLD OF PROFESSIONAL PET SITTING
Pet Sitters International
Pet Sitter of the Year

Carol Proffitt, President
PawPrints Pet Care Corp., USA
Knoxville, TN
(See page 5)

1995 In 1995, *The WORLD* was printed quarterly and added color to its pages. Issues were 12-14 pages in length. It had already become one of the most important benefits of PSI membership. Then, as now, pet sitters relied on the publication for educational information and pet-care tips from other pet sitters.

1996 *The WORLD* continued its quarterly publication, but increased in size to 20 pages per issue. Here is an article from PSI headquarters that is just as applicable to today's pet-sitting industry at it was more than a decade ago.

THE WORLD OF PROFESSIONAL PET SITTING
Be Wise!!

Know Bird Basics for Pet Sitters
(see page 4)

Bonded * Insured * Accredited
by Bill Foster (Summer 1996)
These are three impressive and responsible words to have printed on your business cards. A few "Early Birds" in our membership will soon be graduating from the Pet Sitting Technician course and adding that word "Accredited" to their business cards and literature.

The PSI Accreditation Program got off to a slow start due to printing delays of course materials. Both PSI and ICS are now ready and eager to hear from you with questions and enrollments! All four PSI Accreditation programs contain educational information that will help elevate your staff and business above and beyond your competition.

The Accreditation Program is an enhancement option of your PSI membership. Wouldn't an educational diploma in the front of your presentation book be much more impressive to a customer than a receipt showing you have paid a business license tax?

1997 **WOW! What a difference a full-color cover makes!** The big news in 1997 was that *The WORLD* began bimonthly publication and added more color. It was also the first year that the Pet Owner's Issue was published for PSI members to distribute to their clients.

1998 *The WORLD* continued to expand and the average issue this year was 32 pages. Plans were in the works for PSI's first *Take Your Dog To Work Day*® and pet sitters were beginning to look outside of traditional pet-sitting visits for additional income sources, including pet transportation, grooming, caring for special-needs pets and even pet parties.

1999 This year brought *The WORLD* to a higher level of expertise and information for PSI members. Thom Somes, president of Pet Tech Inc., pet first aid education; and Phil Pearsall, president of Business Insurers of the Carolinas, debuted bimonthly columns in its pages. Both have contributed much invaluable info to PSI members in the past 5 years, such as the following:

Small Business Forum: Insurance Issues
by Phil Pearsall
Business Insurers of the Carolinas
(May/June 1999)

Whenever you have an incident that you feel might result in liability on your part as a pet sitter, please notify our agency immediately. With timely reporting of an incident, the insurance company's adjuster will have an opportunity to investigate the circumstances while the information is fresh on everyone's mind.

A lengthy delay in filing may cause the insurance carrier to refuse to represent you because they were unable to investigate the incident in a timely manner. We had a claim that wasn't reported until eight months after the actual incident occurred. On this claim there were lawsuit papers served on the pet sitter requesting $1 million in damages! These suit damages must be answered to the court with which they were filed within 30 days. The court papers were never sent to our agency. When there is no reply to a suit, the court will automatically award the claimant the amount requested. If the insurance company is not notified about the suit, they will not be responsible for any award granted; therefore the pet sitter will bear the entire financial obligation. So you can see how important timely filing is!

What's Inside

From pet care to office procedures, from behavioral issues to business practices, from health concerns to advice columns, *The WORLD* has brought it all into the homes of PSI members. We hope you will enjoy this look back—and not only enjoy it, but learn from the time honored, proven wisdom that filled the pages of *The WORLD* back then—as it continues to do today.

Section I: Pet Care

Bird Care
Kitty Care

Bird Care

The majority of pet sitters grew up with dogs and cats, but most have gained their knowledge and experience in the care of our feathered friends later in life. And for many PSI members, *The WORLD* was a valuable source of information on avian care.

PSI has been lucky to have Diane Grindol, owner of Avian Images of Pacific Grove, CA, to serve as our foremost expert in avian care. Diane is an avian expert who has written and spoken extensively on the topic of bird care. She has served as a freelance contributor to PSI's Accreditation program and as a *Quest* speaker as well. Her contributions started in 1996 and continue to this day. Her *WORLD* articles are still requested by pet sitters. Here we reprint some of her valuable information about caring for birds.

Bird Care Q & A

by Diane Grindol, Avian Images, Pacific Grove, CA

Summer 1996 Vol. III, Issue 3

Q: What is the minimum number of pet care visits a bird should have? I've had requests to visit every three days.

A: Because it is necessary for a bird to have fresh water available, I would recommend daily visits as a minimum. Birds are especially susceptible to the bacterial illnesses, and bacteria is exactly what likes to grow in water bowls and produces "slime." Many birds end up with droppings or food in their water bowls by design (mischievous parrots) or by accident. The growth of poop soup is not a good thing!

Another good point about daily visits by a pet sitter is that the house is better protected, with daily activity and mail and paper collection. In addition, birds are one of the more social pets. They relish human companionship and activity, which a pet sitter can supply to some extent.

Fall 1996 Vol. III, Issue 4

Q: Can I place my parrot outside on small trees for sunshine and fun? His wings are clipped. Will this expose him to other bird ailments and problems? Many of my clients do this while they are outside with their birds.

A: Do you want the good news or the bad news first?

OK, good news first. Many people take their birds outside for both sunshine and fun. The benefit of putting a bird in the sun is that it produces Vitamin D3, which helps with the absorption of calcium. This benefit cannot be obtained from sunshine coming through a windowpane or acrylic. Many owners make outside stands for their birds from tree branches cemented in a bucket or other large container. Another fun thing for birds outside is playing in a tree – chewing leaves, bark and limbs, or climbing. Non-toxic trees include unsprayed fruit trees (except cherry), willow, eucalyptus and oak. Smaller birds outside in cages can enjoy watching the world go by and visiting with wild birds.

However, here is the bad news. There is some risk in having birds outside and it can't be recommended for the more streamlined birds, like cockatiels or small conures, that fly well even if severely clipped. More bad news is that a bird outside is at risk of being attacked by a predator. This could range from a cat to a hawk or a passing human. You would not want to leave a bird outside unattended. I have had cockatiels outside in a cage contract bird lice. These are harmless, species-specific pests that were easily taken care of with a spray. A more serious health threat to birds is psittacosis (also called chlamydiosis or ornithosis or "parrot fever"), but the possibility is fairly remote they could get it, except by ingesting poop from a wild bird or pigeon. Keep food offered outside covered.

It should be stressed that a bird outside in the sun should be able to get to a shaded part of a cage or have access to shade in case it gets overheated. One of the mysteries of "birdom" brought up by a world authority on macaws, Joanne Abramson, is why do macaws with bare skin patches not get sunburned? I've wondered about that ever since she mentioned it. Still, we must be aware of heat. An overheated bird sticks its wings out from its body, slims down its feathers and pants. It can be sprayed with water to cool down, or in extreme cases, you may use rubbing alcohol on the feet.

And finally, birds are very attune to danger. When they are frightened, they try to fly. It is important to keep wings clipped and to keep checking those wings if a bird goes outside. An extra feather can make a difference in flying ability. Many pet birds become disoriented when outside their home and they don't know how to get down from trees, even if they want to.

I leave the choice up to you. Knowing the risks, you can minimize them by supervising your bird, keeping it clipped and not having food bowls in the open. Knowing the benefits, you can decide if it's worth the risk.

Bird Basics for Pet Sitters
by Diane Grindol

February 1996 Vol. III Issue 1
and May 1996 Vol. III Issue 2

After dogs and cats, birds are the most popular pets in the United States. There was an explosion in their popularity beginning around 1980 to the early 1990s. That popularity has evened out, and the source of pet birds has changed from imported birds to tamer, healthier, domestically raised chicks. With so many people owning birds, there is a definite need for pet sitters who can offer knowledgeable care of birds.

Nuts and Bolts of Bird Sitting

I spoke recently with a pet sitter whose business is about 25 percent bird care. Shawnon Hararah of Pet Watchers in Campbell, California, shared some of her experience with me. She says her clients usually have one or two birds, some have three or four, and a few keep birds in aviaries. For rates, she has three categories of bird (small, medium or large) and charges the same fee for a large bird that she charges to care for a dog. Aviaries are also priced on a small, medium or large basis with the fee to care for a large aviary being comparable to her charge for pet sitting a dog.

Shawnon educated herself about birds because she owned one. She read books and spoke at length to her avian veterinarian. Some things she learned as she went along. She knows how to handle major emergencies, such as a broken blood feather, and has a good relationship with the local avian veterinarian. She has a separate sheet of paper besides her standard contract, which she uses for bird owners. On this she makes good notes regarding the bird's care. Does the bird take regular baths? Does it have clipped wings? Does it go outside? Shawnon is a strong advocate for birds spending time in the sun to absorb vitamin D. In addition, she is also aware of the possibility of disease transmission between birds. Vaccines have not been developed for major bird diseases yet, and some bird diseases are transmitted by airborne particles that can cling to clothing or shoes. As a precaution, Shawnon changes shirts between bird sits. She stuffs a "used" shirt in a plastic bag and washes it when she gets home. When caring for a client's bird in her own home, Shawnon is careful to isolate it from her own pet.

Shawnon finds that she does a lot of client education for bird owners about diet and care, she is always on the lookout for "gifts" to leave clients, like catalogs of quality bird products, pet newsletters, vet business cards and subscription forms to magazines, etc.

Birds are Different

Birds are different in many ways from dogs and cats, a few of which include the following:

Senses. We get used to dealing with dogs and cats with excellent noses. Sniffing a stranger is part of their protocol for greeting, and we are constantly reminded of a dog's sense of smell when out for a walk. Birds, on the other hand, have highly developed eyesight and learn much about their world from visual cues. Birds can see in color, and will react to color and dress. I used to care for my birds in a white bathrobe. The day I switched to a multi-colored robe, my birds reacted with fear, as though they didn't know me! On the positive side, a bird can be provided with colorful toys to be entertained and a bowl of colorful fruits and veggies as both a snack and entertainment.

The species of birds we keep as pets don't see well in the dark. Overnight, birds usually don't vocalize, eat or move about a great deal.

Birds seem to hear fairly well, and vocalizations are important to them to stay in touch with their flock members, define territory and greet the dawn. Anyone who has been associated with a cockatoo probably will never forget the incredible cacophony of a joyous cockatoo! A single male canary sings its song to stake out a territory. That is why a pair of canaries might not be vocal, and why there are certain times of the year a canary does not sing.

Birds have fewer taste buds than we do. The average parrot has about 350 while the average person has about 9,000. This explains why a dried chili pepper is a treat for birds while the same would bring tears to our eyes!

Of course one of the incredible facets of bird vocalizations is that they can say words! This ability varies among species and individuals. Some people claim that birds only "mimic" what they hear with no understanding, but many bird owners report birds that use words at appropriate times. You shouldn't discount any bird's talking ability because of its size, either. The bird reported to have the largest vocabulary in the world is a male budgie—a common American parakeet. Puck is in the 1995 Guinness Book of Records with a vocabulary of more than 1,700 words! Male parakeets have often been reported with large vocabularies rendered in a fast, high-pitched voice. African greys usually mimic sounds and words most clearly, and can often use different "voices" reflecting the speech patterns of the people who taught them. Another surprising talker is the starling! Starlings are not native to the United States, but were imported from England and thus legal to keep as pets. Many pet birds from cockatiels to conures to Eclectus parrots and lories can say at least a few words. To make a bird feel at home, you probably want to find out, as a bird sitter, what words your avian charge does know.

Natural Reactions. Birds are prey animals in the wild. Our dog and cat pets are descended from predators and still have instincts to hunt. They wouldn't have much to fear in the wild. How could a cat sleep 20 hours out of the day if it did! Birds, on the other hand, are alert, and their reaction to stimuli is one of "flight or fright." I have to be careful not to frighten my cockatiels by letting any objects loom above their heads. Balloons at an animal fair or a dust mop taking down cobwebs signal a fear reaction, as though a hawk were hunting above them. When I clip canary toenails, the bird goes totally limp, prepared to be dinner. Parrots don't generally go totally limp, but scream, and a scared cockatiel or budgie will bite hard.

A bird is built to be aware of its environment. It has eyes on both sides of its head for a wide field of vision and reacts to changes. This includes changes in placement of furniture, routine, food or whatever. It's something to keep in mind!

Birds and other Pets. Many people who love pets have a bird and an assortment of other pets as well. There are a few safety considerations to keep in mind.

If a bird in your care should ever be bitten or scratched by a cat, it should be taken to a veterinarian immediately. Cats have bacteria in their mouths that multiplies wildly in birds, and can kill a bird in as little as 24 hours. Any time a cat breaks the skin on a bird is an emergency situation.

Reptiles, which are increasingly popular pets, can carry salmonella bacteria. This affects both birds and people. Be sure to wash your hands thoroughly after handling a reptile. Don't let a reptile hang around areas where food is prepared. If you are caring for both birds and reptiles; take care of the bird first to avoid contamination.

Rodent droppings are full of gram negative bacteria, which could cause infection in birds. A bird's normal flora is gram positive bacteria. Sometimes guinea pigs, rats and birds get along without hostility, but if a bird started pecking at a rodent's litter or droppings, it could become ill. It is best not to allow that close association.

Finally, it seems obvious, but both cats and dogs are natural predators and birds are prey. The species should be closely supervised when they are together. Various households are able to form degrees of friendship or tolerance among the species. You should be aware of potential problems and be able to separate the species appropriately.

Veterinary Care. One of the important things you will want to know as a bird sitter is the names of local avian vets. Birds have very different needs from dogs and cats. Get referrals from area breeders or pet stores, or talk to bird owners. Find out what the avian vet advises for emergencies during hours his or her clinic is closed. You may also ask the Association of Avian Veterinarians (P.O. Box 811720, Boca Raton, FL 33481 or www.aav.org) for the names of vets in your area who have an interest in birds.

There are a couple phone numbers to keep in mind when you cannot get local help. There is a telephone avian veterinary consulting service available. The fee is $2.95 per minute. It is staffed by Dr. Branson Ritchie 7-10 p.m. daily, EST, at (900) 288-4267.

I also keep the animal poison hotline number posted near my phone. There is a fee for this service. Call either (900) 680-0000 or (800) 548-2423.

Domestication. Most animal behaviorists agree that bird keepers are keeping wild animals. We should respect that and realize that a bird's behavior is very much influenced by instincts, meant to ensure its survival in the wild. At this point in time, some birds in captivity were literally taken from the rain forests. There were huge numbers of birds imported into this country during the 1980s. Some of these imported birds were acquired by bird breeders who now offer tame, hand fed baby birds to bird owners. Many species are representatives of the first one-to-three generations bred in captivity.

Birds Represent Many Species – Not Breeds

One of the things I have always loved about dogs is the incredible selection of sizes, shapes and assortment of colors and temperaments available. This is even more remarkable when you consider that, technically, dogs are one species. The variety is in the form of breeds, but all are descended from wolf or jackal ancestors to the best of our knowledge. With the advancement of DNA technology, we might find out differently!

Birds represent a wide variety of species that originated in different geographic areas of the world. They are adapted to live in their particular environment and to fill a role in the ecosystem. Lories have brush tongues to drink nectar from flowers. Cockatiels and parakeets are native to the arid desert of inland Australia. No wonder they make forgiving pets for children and first-time bird owners! Blue and gold macaws are treetop dwellers from the rain forests of the Amazon. In their native habitat they are rained on daily and forage on a wide variety of foods. I have personally visited the habitat of yellow-naped Amazons in Guatemala and listened to the vocalizations of pairs settling down at sunset in the tropics. They have voices that carry for miles. Why do we try to make apartment pets of these creatures?

I'm digressing! The important thing to get out of this is that no one can give you any one set of instructions for caring for birds. Hopefully, you will work with informed owners who know something about the needs of species they are keeping. That way they can provide you with nectar for lories, fruits and veggies for rain forest birds or pinkie mice for a hornbill.

The closest thing to a domesticated bird is the common parakeet, cockatiel or canary. Both zebra finches and society, or Bengalese finches are also common birds that breed willingly. When *BIRD TALK* magazine does surveys of their readership, about 75 percent of their readers own a parakeet or a cockatiel. These species come in a variety of colors, which have been developed in captivity. They have been kept in captivity for some time. Both the parakeet and cockatiel were first imported into the United States in the early 1900s, and were bred in Europe for half a century before that.

The canary has been kept for so long as a songbird that there are breeds of canary. The wild canary is a serin finch you wouldn't take any more notice of than a sparrow or house finch. Far from being all yellow Tweety birds, canaries come in colors from apricot to blue or white, and in variations in feathering. Glosters look like they are wearing hats, Norwich are called "teddy bears" for their stout conformation and the frills look like they dried their feathers in a strong wind. Some breeds were bred for song, and still others for color or conformation.

Longevity

Some of the larger parrot species have life spans equal to that of a human. Macaws and cockatoos have been reported to live to 70 or 80 years old. Canaries and budgies may live as long as 12-15 years, and cockatiels to age 20 and beyond. Amazons, greys and conures probably live about 25-35 years. Pet birds are getting better care than ever before, so as the current generation of birds matures, we will know more about life span in captivity. Obviously, though, there are many larger birds that will live with a family for a generation or two!

Physiology

A bird's anatomy is built for flight. It has hollow bones, and a system of air sacs throughout its body, which makes it lightweight. What this means to you as a pet sitter, is that birds are very susceptible to fumes or smoke. You shouldn't smoke around a bird or use cleaning products near a bird. While we breathe in with two lungs, a bird fills air sacs and bones with the air it takes in. Just remember the canaries in mines that warned miners of toxic fumes before they were affected. (I am told miners were often able to rescue the canaries and take them out the mines with them.)

A bird does not have a diaphragm. If you hold a bird firmly around its middle, you will suffocate it. It would be a good idea to learn how to hold a bird to restrain it in ways that are safe for both you and the bird. It is common to hold a bird with a towel when restraining it.

Birds have feathers. That is one of their most beautiful features, until you have to sweep up a bucketful of them! At certain times of the year birds molt, replacing all the feathers on their body with new ones. It doesn't happen all at once, but rather over a series of weeks. This is a twice-yearly event with my cockatiels, but only once a year for many species. Molting may also be triggered by keeping a bird in an overheated house, by a move or stress.

There are a couple things to keep in mind about birds during molt. New feathers have a blood supply at their base. If the new feather is broken off for some reason, the shaft must be pulled out. It may require the assistance of a veterinarian to do so. If the feather were not pulled out, the bird would continue to bleed. This is another example of a potential emergency situation. Having some emergency supplies on hand is a good idea! Consult with an avian vet but recommended supplies include: aseptic hand washes, two sizes of sterile gauze pads, antiseptic prep pads, styptic pencil for bleeding, forceps for removing blood feathers and Gatorade for fluid replacement.

Sex is a Guess
Another difference in the anatomy of birds is their lack of external sexual organs. This means a bird owner may not know the sex of his or her pet, and that there are not yet safe neutering procedures for birds. Both males and females have gonads (sex organs) in their bodies. Birds can be sexed by a veterinarian, who does minor surgery to look at these gonads, or by submitting blood to a DNA test lab. Because they are not ever neutered, some birds have hormonal and mood fluctuation at certain times of the year when they would be breeding if they were with a mate. For your information, birds raise their babies as pairs and usually both parent the offspring. The notion of a stud bird will make most breeders laugh!

Eating Like a Bird
Most well-educated bird owners these days realize that seed is not a complete diet for their birds.

There are now "pellets" on the market containing vitamins and minerals— just like there are kibbles for dog and cat owners. Birds usually also appreciate an assortment of fruits and vegetables daily, and occasional treats of warm pasta snacks, seeds or nuts. This of course varies by species! You will encounter bird owners feeding seeds (and ideally supplementing those with vitamins, a corn/bean/rice mash or a diet based on sprouted seed and legumes.) The above applies to most parrots. If you are caring for lorries, they are nectar and fruit eaters, while hornbills consume pinkie mice regularly. A basic guide in bird feeding is that birds can eat almost anything people should eat. That means avoid salt, sugar, fat, alcohol and caffeine. They usually love veggie and grain treats. In addition, don't let a bird nibble on avocado or chocolate, both of which are poisonous.

Obedience Training

Birds are intelligent and can understand some commands and "no." However, training or punishment should never be physical with a bird. Bird training and behavior modification are built on a foundation of trust. Good ways to win over a bird include feeding it a favorite treat, talking to it or scratching its head or under its wings. The bird's owner can tell you how it is used to being handled, if at all. Some birds willingly come up onto a hand, arm or stick.

Bird Care Questions to Ask Owner

Some other behavior questions to ask owners include: Does the bird have a favorite toy? Does the owner cover the cage at night? Does the bird know any commands like "up"? What is the bird's diet?

Hopefully you have been inspired to learn more about birds, and even to consider caring for our feathered friends. If you have any questions or comments, please write to me in care of the *The WORLD*!

Kitty Care

In America today, felines are the most common companion animals—and many pet owners have more than one cat. Three to four cats are very common and it is not unusual for cat lovers to have more than four cats in their homes. Multiple-cat households are one big reason that cats make excellent candidates for in-home care by professional pet sitters.

However, cats are, by nature, more difficult to care for than some other household pet species. Cats are the most territorial of domestic pets and they dislike changes to their routines, which can mean special challenges for pet sitters. That is why Kitty Care is an ever-popular topic in the pages of *The WORLD*. Our feline experts are always in high demand and the following articles demonstrate why.

Cultivating Cat Lovers

by Carole Rexer, Cat Care by Carole, Houston, TX

July/Aug 1999 Vol VI, Issue 4

Cat lovers usually own two or more felines. They are willing to spend money for quality pet care. True feline fanatics are searching for the *best care* for their cats at reasonable rates, not just the cheapest available care.

Cat lovers are worth cultivating as clients for many reasons. One important reason is that caring for felines is not physically taxing for pet sitters—Cats don't have to be taken for walks. Since most cats are confined in the home sitters can stay out of weather extremes. It can be a relaxing break in a hectic day. Another advantage of pet sitting for felines is that late evening calls are rare.

It is now 5+ years since I began commercially pet sitting. In researching this article, I asked some of my best clients what they expected in a cat sitter. In addition to reliability and honesty, these **Big Three** qualities were constantly mentioned:

1. Must like cats and feel comfortable with them. Many cat lovers believe that cats are thought of as "second class citizens" of the pet world. They worry their cats won't receive as much time and attention as other animals due to the mythology of feline "independence." At a national pet sitters' conference several years ago, I heard a pet sitter say, "The cats don't notice if I run in and out when I'm in a hurry. All they really care about is if someone feeds them and scoops the litter box." This is the kind of thinking that sends chills up the spines of cat owners. "Independent" does not mean anti-social. Instead, reassure cat owners that your pet-sitting visits feature interactive play. State that playing "Laser Light Tag" or "Catch-da-Bird" gets even the biggest couch potato cats into motion. When speaking to cat owners, it is important to express admiration for the cat's unique characteristics. I've read that "cat people" enjoy owning a pet that is a little different. They appreciate feline "independence" and know it is not "indifference." Cat owners usually are secure individuals who are comfortable with a pet that can never be dominated. In fact, a cat's rejection of human control is often the trait they admire most!

2. Must be knowledgeable about feline health and behavior. There is much misinformation and ignorance about felines. Even many cat owners who really love their kitties are fairly ignorant about their health and behavior. *Cat Watch*, the excellent feline newsletter published by Cornell University College of Veterinary Medicine, recently stated that up until 1983 veterinarians were generally taught to treat cats like smaller dogs. It is not surprising that cats continue to seem like mysterious creatures to so many people. When cat owners phone you to discuss sitting needs, tell them how essential it is that food intake and litter box usage is monitored daily. Dropping cat trivia into a conversation with prospective clients is another method to show them you care enough about cats to have educated yourself on their health and behavior.

3. Must have good litter box maintenance. There is no subject dearer to the hearts of cat owners and their cats than litter box maintenance. I have acquired new clients over the years that have quit using other pet sitters they have been satisfied with in every way—except for the manner with which the litter boxes were dealt. I proclaim *Cat Care by Carole* features *immaculate litter box maintenance!* Litter is always swept up from the floor so that it won't get tracked through the house. Litter is shaken out of rugs under boxes. Advertise that your service specializes in excellent litter box maintenance. I guarantee it will attract cat-loving clients! A word of caution —Be sure to live up to your words. Remember, the day you are in a hurry and do not scoop and sweep thoroughly is sure to be the day clients will arrive home unexpectedly early.

Extra Touches - Little Things Mean A Lot
Every day when pet sitting, I do a "hairball patrol" throughout the house. Dealing with accidents sooner rather than later helps to prevent stains from setting. It also means keeping an eye on the culprit throwing up. (Chronic vomiting can indicate a medical problem.) I don't use any product to clean up stains that the client has not left specifically for me to use. Secondly, I carry a little rubber curry brush. It's a marvelous tool for getting up cat hair from furniture, pillow, rugs and clothes. It actually works better than those rollers with sticky paper for removing cat hair from clothes. Finally, I buy gallon size clear plastic storage bags wholesale from a local grocery store. On my last visit to a client's home, I bag every pooper-scooper. It ensures there is a handy bag for the client to scoop into. It has become one of Cat Care by Carole's business hallmarks. Also, on my last visit, if the house smells musty I spray a bit of air freshener near the door.

Cats, Cats, and More Cats.
Cats have become more numerous as pets than dogs. There are more dog owners, but cat lovers tend to own multiple felines. Cats are perceived as being an easier pet to maintain and less expensive to care for than dogs. Cat ownership continues to increase. Because cat owners are more likely to own multiple kitties, I recommend that pet sitters charge by the amount of time required caring for them rather that charging by the number of cats. It is important to advertise that if the pet owner has two or more felines, they may *save* money by using a professional pet sitter instead of boarding their cats. If possible on brochures, flyers and ads, have room devoted exclusively to cats. Advertise how your service cherishes kitty clients and emphasize the special care you offer. All of my ads (including my Web site) state, "I love and understand cats!"

Cat lovers present a lucrative market for pet sitters to tap. I believe it is an under-served market. There are many cat owners now using friends and neighbors to check on their cats, but with proper marketing strategy and a commitment to giving cat owners *exactly* what they want in pet sitting, those cat lovers can become loyal clients.

Shy Kitties Become Pet Sitting Nightmare!

by Dawn Secord Fur, Feathers & Fins LLC, Chino Hills, CA

July/August 1999 Vol VI, Issue 4

Editor's Note:
How often have you heard a client say, "My cat is shy, so don't worry if you don't see him during your visit?" Do those words unnerve or terrify you?"A member shares her experience with "shy kitties."

I recently interviewed with a client who planned a six-week trip to Europe. She and her husband had two cats that primarily lived in the garage. They were "inside only" cats. One cat was very interactive and the other cat was hiding. The owner retrieved the "shy" Russian blue and told us that he tends to hide in the garage and "not to worry if you don't see him."

On my first visit, the Russian blue was no where in sight. The garage door was closed, not ajar as the client normally left it. I always make sure to see each pet, even if they choose not to be interactive, in order to make sure they are medically OK. I, accompanied by my husband and another pet sitter, began to search for the hidden cat. Fifteen minutes turned into thirty. Just how many places in a garage can a cat hide? Let me tell you, a ton of them! Then we searched the house, room by room, closet by closet, leaving every door open in case he had been trapped inside. Our search was now 45 minutes long, multiplied by three people searching in every direction. We could not find him! I grudgingly went to the phone to call our new client in Europe. She started crying when I explained.

After the call, I went out to look around the yard, under the bushes, around the fence. No sign of kitty. Then I searched the trash cans...and found one extremely frightened fatboy wedged up between two cans. The cat was so scared; he was fairly placid when I scooped him up. Back inside,

 we gave him water, left him to his litterbox, and spent time rubbing and caressing him. He had been out for almost 24 hours. I called the client back and her delight warmed my heart. She said the cat must have snuck out when her husband took out the trash. A happy ending, but I will continue to always, always, always locate each pet during a visit, even when the owner says it's OK not to!

Animal Behavior
Vets on Pets

Animal Behavior

Animal behavior is a vast field. And, while understanding pets and their behavior is best learned by actually handling, working and caring for them, much can be accomplished through reading. *The WORLD* has offered advice columns and in-depth features on behavior problems—and thousands of pet sitters and their clients have benefited from them.

Knowledge of animal behavior is a two-sided coin for pet sitters—and a very valuable one! Not only will this knowledge help a sitter safely perform pet-sitting duties, but it can also benefit the pet owners and the pets themselves. Many animals that exhibit behaviors their owners can't deal with end up in animal shelters. In fact, behavior problems top the list of reasons for pet relinquishment. In addition, thousands of other pets are given up because of lifestyle changes, such as the birth of a child or human health issues. When a pet sitter can help clients understand their pets and aid in correcting behavior problems, everyone wins.

Interdog Aggression

by Claire Newick, RVT, CCS Member Association of Pet Dog Trainers

July/August 1999, Volume VI, Issue 4

Editor's Note: In response to another PSI member's experience in trying to break up a dog fight, Claire Newick offered this advice.

While I agree that throwing water on quarrelling dogs is a sound first step to halting a fight, I disagree on separating fighting dogs by grabbing their collars. Pet sitters should **never** get their hands anywhere near the mouths of dogs in the heat of battle. A better method is to grab both rear legs of one dog and walk backwards. Sometimes all that is necessary to halt a dogfight is to break eye contact. When I am walking dogs known for interdog aggression and see a potential quarrel, I turn the dog in the opposite direction so it can't see the other dog. Hopefully, this is all it takes for the dog to forget its aggression.

When I train dogs, I tell clients that whatever emotions they feel are transferred through the leash to the dog. If the owner is fearful or apprehensive with another dog approaching, the dog will pick up that vibe and behave accordingly. A better method is to take a "no big deal" attitude. Pet sitters should remain calm, break the eye contact by turning around or crossing the street, tell the dog, "Stop it, heel, and let's go." They shouldn't walk dogs with only a buckle collar and I never recommend using retractable leashes. I keep several lengths of choke chains and 6-ft. nylon leashes handy.

Nothing takes the place of early socialization. The critical socialization period agreed on by most experts is 6-16 weeks of age. This is a window of opportunity to expose the dog to other dogs, thunderstorms (buy a CD), people of different races, children, hats, uniforms, household noises, wheelchairs, canes, etc.

Dogs are pack animals and there is a leader in every group. The human owner should be the ultimate alpha dog, but this is not always the case. Subordinate dogs sometimes fight for a higher position in social standing. Interdog aggression escalates when dogs reach sexual maturity (it doesn't matter if the animals are spayed or neutered), usually 2-3 years old. This explains how dogs raised together can suddenly hate each other and start fighting. Fighting is worst between female dogs. If a client asks, I recommend a male with another male or a male and a female. Female dogs fight to the death and should not be put in the same household.

It is important for pet sitters to recognize and respect the canine social hierarchy. Once the alpha dog is identified, it should be petted first, fed first, etc. Paying attention to the beta or lower members of the group first will upset the balance and may lead to resentment by the alpha dog. Most pet sitters have policies against sitting for aggressive dogs. As a precaution, all the pet sitters should receive tetanus shots, which are good for ten years. As much as pet sitters enjoy caring for dogs, we need to be aware of canine aggression and deal with incidents as they arise.

Survey Said...

Here is some PSI member feedback on avoiding or handling dog fights.

- I try to watch the dogs carefully the first few days I'm with them. That way I know which ones are more likely to fight. I keep aggressive dogs on leash when around other dogs. *A. Verdone, Pawfect Pet Sitters, Oregon. WI*

- Separate dogs by crating them. When things calm down, let them out. Watch to make sure they stay calm. *Scruffy and Friends, Bentonville, AR*

- Keep dogs on leashes and walk them only in daylight. Use pepper spray, warm or cold water to break up fights. *K. Deisenroth, Moments of Caring, Elkhart, IN*

- I keep an electronic buzzer with me. Humans can't hear it, but it distracts dogs. Use cold water and blankets or a sheet to disengage fighting dogs. *Pat Culver's Pet Care, Rochester, NY*

- When walking dogs, I carry a small squirt bottle of vinegar and water to signal "Off!" *Evelyn Zanella, Enterprises; Cambria, CA*

- When clients ask that certain pets be kept separate, I respect this and keep them apart at all times. *Pets Are People Too, Hephzibah, GA*

- Feed them separately. Give the alpha dog attention first. If dogs are fighting, don't get between them. Grab their hind legs and pull them apart. *Furry Friends, Lafayette, LA*

- If two people are present, have each lift a dog by the hind legs. If only person is present, try· to identify the dog that won't back down and lift that one's hind legs. *C. Hoffer, Canina Campovers, Boulder, CO*

- Use a clean, dry soda can with 10 pennies in it to shake. Follow with a loud "No!" or a shot of water. *Precious Pets, Sacramento, CA*

Dog and Cat Bites – Key Facts for Pet Sitters

by C. Wayne Lankford, M.D., Pilot Mountain Family Practice, Pilot Mountain, NC

May/June 1999 Vol. IV, Issue 3

At least 10,000 people are hospitalized each year in the United States for dog or cat bites. No firm estimate of the total number of bites is possible, since many bites are not reported or are less serious and are cared for at home. A pet sitter is at high risk for adding to these statistics, often caring for an animal he or she does not know at a time when the animal is away from its people. The sitter is often "invading" the animal's home and is at increased risk for attack. Common sense and a few precautions can lessen the risk. But if bitten, the sitter should have a basic knowledge of what to do.

Common-sense precautions include being calm and quiet around a new animal. Try to limit the number of new people introduced to the animal. Leave animals alone while they eat. Avoid animals if they are acting strange or appear sick. In such situations, if possible, seek care for them from someone they may know better than you do. Do not try to separate fighting animals. Keep children away from animals not familiar with small humans. The pet's owner will be able to tell you the DOs and DON'Ts particular to their pet. The sitter should also obtain from the owner any history of previous attacks and the pet's rabies immunization status.

If, despite the best precautions, the sitter is bitten, the animal should be contained to prevent further risk to the sitter. Dog bites tend to be more serious and damaging than cat bites, since dog teeth and jaws are designed for crushing and tearing. Despite the heavier damage usually inflicted, fewer dog bites than cat bites become infected. Cats have fine, sharp teeth that cause deep puncture wounds and contaminate the wound with bacteria from the cat's mouth and from the surface of the victim's skin. Most wounds will show redness, pain, heat and drainage associated with infection within 24 hours of the bite. Scratches by cats or dogs are usually not a problem unless they later become infected.

Wound care should first include gentle washing with large amounts of soap and water. Apply pressure with a clean towel or washcloth to control bleeding. Try not to use paper products since they will stick in the wound. Apply a clean dressing, then, if the wound is on an arm or leg, elevate the wound above the level of the heart to decrease swelling. The bite should be reported—usually to the local health department or animal control.

You should seek a doctor's care immediately if you have persistent pain, numbness around the wound, obvious deformity of the tissues or visible bone or tendon within the wound. All deep cat bites should be seen because of the high risk of infection. Dog bites of the hand, foot or head are serious and should be treated immediately. Any deep or gaping wound will require surgical treatment. Generally, wounds should be stitched within six-to-eight hours of the injury to decrease the risk of infection. You must be seen if you cannot control the bleeding.

Sitters with diabetes, cancer, AIDS, liver or lung disease, those taking steroids or having any other situation which suppresses the immune system are particularly susceptible to certain bacteria found in dog and cat bites, and can die from severe infections. Cat-Scratch Disease can be contracted from cats *or* dogs and leads to swelling of lymph nodes within several days of a bite or scratch. If the sitter has not had a tetanus shot within 5 years, a booster may be needed.

If the rabies immunization status of the pet is unknown, it is imperative that the animal be contained and observed, especially if the pet has outdoor access. Animal control must be notified to assist in decisions regarding appropriate treatment for possible rabies exposure.

Hopefully, most sitters will never need these wound instructions. For those unfortunates who are bitten, I hope this article will assist you in obtaining appropriate care.

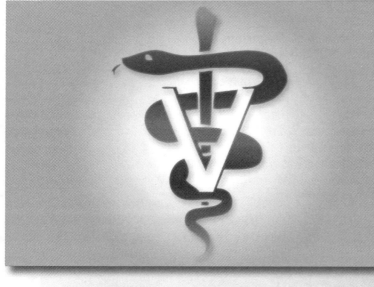

Vets on Pets

Dr. Lynn Roberts began advising pet sitters in the very first issue of *The WORLD*. Since that time, she has provided pet sitters with invaluable pet-care information through her "Vets on Pets" and "Ask the Vet" columns. She continues to serve as one of PSI's most valuable resources on pet health care.

Aggressive Animals

by Lynn Roberts, DVM Animal Care Clinic, Rural Hall, NC

May 1994 Vol. 1 Issue 1

It is the rare person in any animal care profession who doesn't eventually encounter an aggressive animal. Pet sitters may have the most difficult job, because they must enter the animal's home (a territorial threat to an aggressive animal) without the presence of the owner. What you do, or don't do, may determine whether or not you are bitten.

Do
- Stand still.
- Command the dog to "Sit" or "Down"
- Face the dog.
- Move slowly.
- Keep quiet.
- Look at the ground. (Never look an aggressive animal in the eye.)

Don't
- Scream or shout.
- Run or move quickly.
- Threaten the dog with an object.
- Stare.
- Extend your hand.

If you are bitten by an animal and it has penetrated the skin (no matter how small), go to your doctor's office immediately. All animals have bacteria in their mouths, and a nasty infection could result from the wound if not properly treated.

Make sure any animal you are pet sitting is current on its rabies vaccine. (This excludes birds, fish or small rodents; ferrets however, should be vaccinated for rabies.) Any bite should be reported to the local health department or animal control office where the animal can then be properly quarantined.

If you have received a bite wound that has penetrated the skin and the animal is not current on its rabies vaccination, you will need to undergo rabies prophylaxis. This is why it is important to report all bite wounds to the proper authorities.

If you find yourself in a situation with an aggressive animal, follow the above rules and leave the premises. It is not worth getting bit or worse. The owner should be contacted and arrangements should be made for the animal to be taken to a kennel or veterinary office where aggressive animals can be handled.

What to Do
If You Are Bitten On the Job

by Lynn Roberts, DVM

March/April 1997 Vol IV Issue 2

Because we cannot always predict the actions of animals, working with them can sometimes be hazardous. One of the things animal care providers fear is being bitten on the job.

A bite from an animal that doesn't penetrate the skin usually doesn't require a doctor's care unless extensive bruising has occurred. Any bite that penetrates the skin needs a doctor's care. Even the tiniest of puncture wounds or scratches can "inject" bacteria beneath the skin's surface. These bacteria can multiply quickly leading to cellulites, abscess or tendon sheath infections (if the bacteria enter the tendon sheath of hands, arms and legs). If the infection is aggressive, hospitalization and intravenous antibiotics may be in order for the "unlucky pet sitter." If the bite is treated immediately, antibiotics and tetanus injection may be all that is needed.

Always check on the aggressive animal's rabies vaccinations status. If the animal is not current on his rabies vaccine, it will need to be quarantined for 10 days and you may need to undergo rabies prophylaxis (a series of five injections during one month).

I urge everyone in the pet care profession to have themselves vaccinated against rabies. These vaccines can be given at the local health department with prior arrangements. The vaccine must be given in a three injection series for a total cost of $150-$175. Remember, rabies can kill. Your life is worth the cost.

Bloat

by Dr. Lynn Roberts, DVM

March/April 1999 Vol IV, Issue 2

Bloat, or distension of the stomach, is caused by accumulation of swallowed air, food, gas and stomach secretions. It is predominately found in large, deep-chested dogs such as Great Danes, Irish setters, Doberman pinchers, German shepherd dogs, Irish wolfhounds and boxers. The age of most cases is between four and seven years, and death can approach 47 to 50 percent. Although more common in large and giant breed dogs, it has also been reported in the Pekingese, dachshund and English bulldog breeds. It can also occur in cats, foxes, rabbits, rats, mice and monkeys.

The exact cause of bloat is unknown, although many associated factors have been incriminated. These include anatomy, exercise after eating, hereditary predisposition, stomach emptying dysfunction and swallowing excessive amounts of air.

It is very important to recognize the signs of bloat so emergency veterinary care can be started immediately. There is usually a sudden onset of restlessness, abdominal pain and excessive salivation (a sign of nausea). These animals usually retch, but are unable to vomit. As the condition worsens, the abdomen becomes distended (these animals often look like they swallowed a basketball). The animal becomes shocky (weak, pale gums, and cold extremities).

Treatment requires stomach decompression and shock correction. Initially, passage of a stomach tube is attempted. If this fails, a needle is placed into the stomach and air is released. A stomach tube is then attempted again. If these procedures fail to decompress the stomach, surgery will be necessary. Shock therapy is critical since many animals will die from complications due to shock, even if stomach decompression is successful.

Since no specific cause of bloat has been identified, control measures may not be successful. However, breeds that are prone to bloat may respond to the following suggestions:

1. Feed multiple small meals over the day instead of a large single meal.

2. Feed moistened foods or foods higher in carbohydrates or protein (rather than high fat content foods) so that the stomach will empty more rapidly.

3. Minimize water consumption after exercise.

4. Minimize exercise after eating.

Bloat is a common problem in susceptible breeds and carries with it a rapid onset of clinical signs and high death rate. Recognizing the signs of bloat is extremely important. Professional assistance should be sought promptly if any animals with suspicious clinical signs are identified under your watch.

How Often Should A Cat Be Visited?

by Lynn Roberts, DVM

February 1995 Vol.II Issue 1

A pet sitter wrote to me last month with a question that I feel warrants an answer. This pet sitter has a client who requests she visit her cats on every third day. The pet sitter was very uncomfortable with this arrangement and asked how often pets should be checked.

Although cats tend to be very self-sufficient, we must always remember that the domesticated cat depends on us for survival. Animals cannot call the doctor when they are sick or injured and cannot medicate themselves. They are dependent upon us for their food and basic well being.

While it is common practice for an owner to leave for the weekend and leave a cat behind with "overflowing" food and water bowls, it could also be dangerous practice. Just last week a lady brought a cat into our hospital. The owner was away on vacation and this person, a friend, was checking on the cat every few days. On this particular day she found the cat in a coma with pools of vomit surrounding it. She rushed the cat to the hospital, where we were able to put the pieces of the puzzle together. The cat had developed a urethral blockage (the tube that connects the bladder to the outside) and could not urinate. The bladder had become very distended and kidney toxins began to poison his bloodstream. If this lady had waited another hour or two, this cat would have died. Fortunately for the cat, we were able to relieve the blockage and place the cat on intravenous fluids. After three days of hospitalization he was doing well.

The point of this story is to remind everyone that anything can happen when an animal is left alone. I always get a barrage of emergency calls between 6:00 p.m. and 7:00 p.m. This is due to owners coming home from work and finding their animals with this problem or that injury. These animals had only been at home alone for 12 hours or less!

My advice would be a set policy to check any animal every day or twice daily. If you decide to let an owner talk you into checking an animal every two or three days, make sure you have it in writing that this goes against your policy and that the owners have been advised that problems can arise when an animal is not checked daily. Remember that when an owner contracts your services you are now responsible for the care of the pet. Should anything happen to the animal, guess who the owner is going to blame?

We are all guilty of letting owners "bully" us into things that make us uncomfortable. We must always remember that by compromising ourselves, we also compromise our reputation and our profession.

Feline Leukemia Virus

By Lynn Roberts, DVM

Jan/Feb 1997 Vol IV Issue 1

This month a pet sitter has asked us to consider any special precautions necessary when pet sitting a cat infected with feline leukemia virus (hereafter referred to as "FeLU").

FeLU is a virus which only infects cats (humans and dogs need not apply). Professors in veterinary colleges often use words like "mean," "nasty" and "sneaky" when describing it, because of the serious and unpredictable nature of the disease. FeLU infection can kill a cat outright by affecting almost any body organ or system. It also causes severe suppression of immune system function, which leaves cats vulnerable to other diseases.

Because FeLU-positive cats become seriously ill, I would definitely have a written agreement with the owner describing his or her wishes for veterinary care should the cat become ill.

A pet sitter's other worry would be the possible transmission of FeLU from the positive cat to FeLU-free cats at his or her "next stop." This is where our thoroughly depressing tale takes on a slightly more positive light. While FeLU is almost impossible to eradicate once it is inside a cat's body and infection has occurred, it survives for only a short time in the environment outside of the cat. Infectious virus particles have been found in blood, saliva, urine and other bodily fluids, but transmission almost always occurs directly from cat to cat during fighting or mating. Repeated and prolonged exposure through mutual grooming, eating from the same dish or sharing a litter box rarely causes infection. Human beings almost never act as vectors of FeLU (carrying the disease from cat to cat) because the virus dies so soon outside of the cat.

Since "almost never" will not be good enough for most of you, there are some precautions you can take after handling a FeLU-positive cat or its "stuff." Diluted Clorox solution (approximately one cup Clorox per gallon of water) will kill virus on hands, shoes, etc. We often change lab jackets as well as disinfecting hands, clean tables, etc., when we treat FeLU-positive cats at work, so, if you want to be doubly sure, change clothes before seeing your next cat client. Also, remember that there is a vaccine for FeLU, which provides good (but not 100 percent) protection, from this disease.

Also, be aware of another cat virus called Feline Immunosuppressive Virus (FIV), which is the feline equivalent of human HIV (AIDS virus). No vaccine as yet exists for this virus, but its transmission and the precautions a pet sitter should take in handling a positive cat are very similar to FeLU.

Caring for Geriatric Pets

by Lynn Roberts, DVM

November 1994 Vol. 1 Issue 3

Due to the short life span of animals, most of you will pet sit for geriatric animals on a routine basis. While dogs and cats begin to undergo these changes starting at age 5 to 7 years, different pets will show the various signs of growing old at different rates. A little more care and responsibility come with sitting for these important family members.

Older dogs and cats have slower metabolisms and therefore have an increasing intolerance to heat and cold. They are producing less of the hormones which are critical for maintaining the body's normal temperature.

With colder weather coming on, I would recommend that owners keep their thermostat at 65 degrees Fahrenheit. For outside dogs and cats, shelter from the wind and cold is a necessity.

Many of you will also note that the older pet may be blind, deaf or both. This means that when letting them outside, close supervision (even in confined areas) is a must! Always avoid moving furniture or familiar objects; i.e., food bowls, water bowls and bedding. Geriatric pets need a consistent routine in their lives.

These pets also tend to have more health problems than their younger counterparts. Therefore, it is very important to always give medication and food on time. This is especially important for the diabetic dog or cat. Always follow the owner's schedule and instructions precisely.

Special diets are common among geriatric animals. Common ailments that require special diets include kidney disease, liver disease, urinary tract problems, allergic disorders and obesity. These diets need to be given strictly with no substitutes. Giving these animals a small "treat" brought from home without the owner's permission could result in dire consequences.

Geriatric patients with kidney disease could pose a special problem for pet sitters. Most of them drink two to three times more water and urinate two to three times more than the normal pet. This may require more visits to allow the pet outside and replenish the fresh water supply to prevent dehydration.

If you find yourself pet sitting for a geriatric pet, make sure the owner has listed all health problems that may be present and provides a thorough list of medications that may need to be given.

Always have their veterinarian's name and phone number available, because geriatric pets are more at risk of health problems while the owner is away than the younger pet.

At Home?..Or At The Vets?

by Lynn Roberts, DVM

May 1995 Vol.II Issue 2

Recently a pet sitter sent me this question, "What health problems should sitters stay away from? When is it best for the pet to be boarded at the veterinarian's?"

Interviewing a client with their pets is the best way to get a feel for a bad situation. The interview allows the owner to discuss the pet's needs, routines, and general care. The interview allows the pet sitter to observe the animal's general well being and care, and any health problems can be discussed at this time.

Any pet with chronic health problems or with a long list of medications should set off warning bells. A pet that has had a recent serious illness should also be interviewed with caution. As long as the pet is stable and its health is not declining or changing, it is probably safe to sit for the animal. Always have the client's veterinarian's name, phone number, and location. Don't forget to have written permission to seek veterinary attention if needed. Animals that need constant monitoring and/or injectable medication are best left in a veterinarian's care. Examples of diseases or conditions in pets I would avoid as a pet sitter include diabetes, uncontrolled epilepsy, asthma, moderate to severe kidney or liver failure, small dogs prone to hypoglycemic (low blood sugar) attacks, animals undergoing chemotherapy or recently blocked male cats. Of course there are many other situations on an individual basis that will require your judgment.

Make sure during the interview that the owner understands his/her pet's illness and possible complications that could arise during his/her absence. Together you should be able to make an educated decision as to the best care for the pet while the owner is away.

If there is any doubt...CALL YOUR VETERINARIAN!

Medicating Pets

by Lynn Roberts, DVM

May/June 1997 Vol IV Issue 3

Unfortunately for pet sitters, many clients will ask you to administer medication to their pets while they are away. While most pets accept medication readily, some may prove to be difficult.

In general, medicating dogs is much easier than medicating cats. The easiest way to give dogs tablets is to hide the pill inside a small amount of food. Commonly used "treats" are canned dog food, cheese, bread, peanut butter or other similar items. If the dog refuses the "medicated treat," gently but firmly open the dog's mouth by placing your hand over his muzzle and your thumb and fingers behind the large canine (fang) teeth on the opposite sides of his mouth. With the other hand, separate the jaws and place the pill as far back on the center of the tongue as possible. Close the dog's mouth and hold it shut. Stroke his throat until he has swallowed. Keep in mind that short-nosed breeds are the most difficult to pill (i.e. Pekinese, Shih Tzu, etc.) and liquid medication is always preferable for these breeds. If you must give a dog liquid medication, insert the dropper between the teeth and cheek and, while tilting the chin upward, slowly dispense the medication.

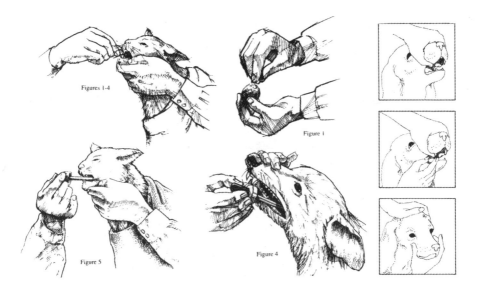

Figures 1-4

Figure 1

Figure 5

Figure 4

Cats rarely accept medication in food (there are exceptions!) and usually need to be "pilled" or given liquid medication. Start by wrapping the cat's body and legs tightly in a towel, leaving only its head sticking out from the towel. Cradle the cat in one arm and place your thumb and forefinger on either side of its face. You can force the mouth open by applying gentle pressure at the space between the teeth. Remember to keep the cat's head tilted up. "Drop" the pill into the cat's mouth. Massage or rub the cat's throat until he or she swallows. Liquid medication is given the same as for dogs.

In pet birds, the addition of medication to drinking water is often the only practical means of drug administration. Oral suspension, ground tablets or the contents of capsules may be applied to fruit, peanut butter sandwiches, fresh corn, cooked sweet potatoes or other items. This generally works best for larger birds such as macaws or parrots.

It's very important to follow directions carefully and make sure you understand how the client wants you to administer the medication. If administration proves too difficult, contact the owner or the veterinarian who prescribed the medication for further instruction.

Rabies

by Lynn Roberts, DVM

August 1995 Vol.II Issue 3

Rabies cases are increasing rapidly and are epidemic proportions in many areas of this country and others. Professional pet sitters need to be completely educated on the rabies virus and how to handle situations in which rabies may be a potential problem.

Rabies is notorious because of its highly fatal nature. This viral disease can affect all warm-blooded animals. Transmission is usually through bite wounds. Infection may also occur by contamination of existing wounds with infected saliva or other infected material. Airborne transmission may also occur. The incubation time is extremely variable and can be as short as 15 days or as long as one year. (Incubation time is the time from the bite until signs of disease occur.) Most affected animals initially undergo behavioral changes. Normally friendly animals may become aggressive and *vice versa*. As the disease progresses, signs noted include biting, changes in voice, slobbering of saliva and dropped lower jaw. Paralysis and convulsions may be seen before death.

I feel it is important that everyone understand the nature of this virus so that situations that pose a rabies risk can be avoided. ***First of all, I would require all clients to have their pets vaccinated for rabies.*** Dogs, cats and ferrets have been approved for vaccination. Type of vaccination and vaccination intervals differ from place to place depending on disease incidence. Foxes, wolves, wolf hybrids, raccoons, skunks and opossums have no approved vaccine protocol for rabies. Because of this, I would hesitate, and in most cases refuse, to pet sit for any client that has these animals as pets. Rabies is very rare in rabbits, squirrels and other small rodents so pet sitting for these species is safe.

In the event you should be bitten by any animal, you should immediately report this not only to your doctor but also to the local health department. The animal needs to be quarantined for 10 days regardless of whether it has been vaccinated for rabies or not. (The quarantine period is 10 days because if an animal is actively shedding virus (i.e. infective), signs of disease will be apparent within 10 days). Just because you are sitting for a house cat or dog who rarely goes outside is not an excuse to ignore the bite. These bites should also be reported. Rabid animals are literally out of their mind and many a raccoon, bat or other animal has gotten into a house and bitten its occupant.

I also recommend that pet sitters or anyone who regularly handles animals get vaccinated for rabies. Your local health department can give you more information about having yourself vaccinated. This is a simple procedure that will go a long way toward helping protect you from this deadly, contagious virus.

What's in a Stool?

by Lynn Roberts, DVM

Jan/Feb 1999 Vol. VI Issue 1

Can looking at the stools of animals give us a clue to possible disease? Yes! Small animal stools (I will deal with dogs and cats in this issue) can vary dramatically in color, consistency and volume. Diets can have a big impact on what stools in most dogs and cats look like. However, most dog and cat stools should be brown (light to dark, depending on diet) and formed (not too loose or too hard).

Most worms and other parasites cannot be seen in animals' stools. The majority of worms and parasites live in the dog's or cat's intestines. Most worms produce eggs that are shed in the feces, but they are microscopic. It requires examination of the feces under a microscope to identify the eggs of individual worms. An exception to this would be tapeworms and, occasionally, roundworms. Tapeworms segment off in the intestines, and the segments look like flat white rice in the stool. These segments can also be found around the anus or attached to the fur around the anus. Roundworms can occasionally be passed in the stool. These worms look like strands of spaghetti.

Fresh red blood in the stool with or without mucous (clear and jelly-like substance) generally indicates a colon (or large intestine) problem. These dogs generally continue to eat well and do not vomit, but diarrhea is usually present. Possible causes of large intestine problems include whipworms, colitis (bacterial or spastic), allergies, inflammatory bowel disease or possible colon cancer.

Dark, tarry-like stools with or without diarrhea indicate bleeding in the stomach or small intestines. The blood appears black and tarry (sticky) because the blood has been digested. These dogs are usually vomiting, experience some weight loss and/or dehydration. Possible causes of stomach or small intestine problems include parasites, bacterial or viral diseases, pancreatitis, inflammatory bowel disease, stomach ulcers, milk intolerance, cancer and others.

Excessively hard, firm or dry feces may be an indication of constipation in dogs and cats. It can be useful to break these stools up and look for hair, bones, rocks or sand. Finding an underlying cause for the constipation can provide an easy treatment for these animals (i.e. hair ball lubricants or removing source in the case of rocks, sand or bones).

Other less-common stool changes to be aware of include gray or chalky stools and stools with excessive amounts of fat in them. Stools that are gray or chalky white may indicate a liver problem. Stools that have excessive amounts of fatty material in them (high volume, very foul odor, and greasy), accompanied by large amounts of flatulence may indicate pancreatic digestive enzyme deficiencies.

When walking dogs or changing litter boxes, pay attention to those stools. You may be able to clue your clients into a problem with their pet that they may have not noticed.

To Vaccinate or Not to Vaccinate?

by Lynn Roberts, DVM

February 1996 Vol. III, Issue 1

Most kennels and veterinary offices require that pets be fully vaccinated before boarding in their facilities. Pet sitters, however, provide a unique service in that in-home care eliminates direct contact of animals from different families. This doesn't completely eliminate the chance of transmission of certain viruses. An important question has arisen as to whether vaccines should be recommended or required of your client's pets.

It is essential that all of your client's pets be vaccinated for rabies. (See Nov. '95 *WORLD* column on the dangers and the specifics of rabies for pet sitters.) This virus is on the rise in the '90s and it kills! Not only have hundreds of animals died recently from rabies, but a number of humans have also died from this non-treatable virus within the past few years. It is also recommended that you have yourself vaccinated for rabies for your own protection. You can contact your local health department for information.

Boarding facilities usually require that all dogs be vaccinated (in addition to rabies) for distemper, hepatitis, leptospirosis, parainfluenze, parvovirus, coronarvirus, and Bordetella. Most of these viruses are passed from dog to dog via direct or airborne transmission. The threat of possible transmission of these viruses increases in boarding facilities because the dogs are housed together. Transmission of most of these viruses by pet sitters is unlikely except for some notable exceptions. Parvovirus (and to a lesser degree coronavirus) is a deadly gastrointestinal virus that affects primarily the very young (<2 yrs.) or the very old (>10 yrs.) dog. The virus is shed in the vomit and the feces. This virus will encapsulate and can survive for very long periods (as long as 1 year) where it has been shed. *A person* walking on ground where this virus is present can pick it up on shoes and clothing, thereby transferring the virus long distances. *Pet sitters should either require or recommend that dogs be vaccinated for parvovirus and coronavirus because you could end up being the reason a puppy gets very sick or dies.*

Vaccines required for cats that board at kennels or veterinary offices (in addition to rabies) include rhinotracheitis, calicivirus, pneumonitis, and panleukopenia. Vaccines that are recommended but usually not required include feline leukemia and feline infectious peritonitis (FIP). Feline leukemia and FIP are spread through direct cat to cat transmission (primarily bite wounds). Rhinotracheitis, calicivirus, and pneumonitis are all respiratory viruses that are spread through airborne transmission. These viruses, therefore, are not likely to be spread by pet sitters. Panleukopenia, however, is a parvovirus and acts similar in all ways to dog parvovirus. Panleukopenia (often referred to as cat distemper) should be recommended or required. Again, you could be a source of transmission from one house to another.

In summary, for total protection all vaccines are always recommended. In particular, pet sitters should either require or recommend in writing that dogs be vaccinated for rabies and parvovirus and cats be vaccinated for panleukopenia. This is not only recommended for obvious health reasons for you and your client's pets but also for legal reasons as well.

Note: Lyme disease is only a problem in a few states in the United States. Check with your veterinarian for information pertaining to it in your area. Parvovirus is a dog virus only and cannot be passed to humans or cats. Panleukopenia is strictly a cat virus.

Vets and Pet Sitters

by Dr. Lynn Roberts, DVM

May/June 1999 Vol IV, Issue 3

Many people would consider pet sitters and veterinarians (especially those who operate boarding facilities) to be natural born enemies. Can a veterinarian ever build a solid working relationship with a pet sitter? The answer is yes.

While the businesses of boarding and pet sitting seem to be inherently in conflict, there are ways in which cooperation and interaction can be mutually beneficial. As a veterinarian, I personally know of animals who are not happy in a boarding kennel. They may be old, anxious, or even a bit crazy. Because the animal's well being is my highest professional concern, I honestly report these problems to the owner and will openly admit that a pet sitter may be the best answer. The owner will often ask his/ her veterinarian to recommend a pet sitter in this situation, and you may receive the referrals from a veterinarian with whom you have a good working relationship.

When a pet owner is new to the area, you may be asked to recommend a doctor for his/her animals. Your recommendation may serve to reward a veterinarian who has referred clients to you. Your veterinarian may also provide advice and technical support for those of you who publish newsletters for your clients.

It is also a great idea for you to be familiar with veterinarians used by your clients. If a pet in your care becomes ill, you need to know the owner's preferences in medical care. Written authorization detailing where to take the pet is very helpful. It is also helpful if the owner has a note placed in his/her pet's medical file explaining that you are authorized to present the animal for treatment. Since emergencies don't occur on schedule, you may also find yourself interacting with the local emergency clinic. A phone call to the supervising veterinarian or office manager may help to establish how charges would be handled in that event.

Taking care of these details in advance makes a tense situation go much smoother. It also demonstrates to your client that you are on the ball concerning his/her pet's care. Lastly, it demonstrates to the veterinarian that you are the sort of proactive, detail-oriented professional that he or she could confidently recommend to a client.

There are many ways in which this relationship may be fostered. If you are a pet owner yourself, your own veterinarian is a great place to start. He or she already knows how much you care about animals by the way you treat yours. You, in turn, have already placed your trust in the doctor for the treatment of your own pets.

Since both professions have the pet's best interest at heart, veterinarians and pet sitters need not be adversaries. Good communication is necessary for both sides. After all, our clients look to us for advice, and we can't recommend one another if we don't know each other.

Zoonotic Diseases

by Lynn Roberts, DVM

May 1996 Vol. III, Issue 2

A zoonotic disease is a disease that can be transmitted from animals to man. The following list includes only a few of the most commonly transmitted diseases. By being aware of potential danger, you can usually avoid becoming ill yourself.

1) **Ringworm**. Ringworm is a fungus that infects the skin of cats and dogs. It causes patches of hair loss, skin crusting, and skin scaling. Direct contact with these lesions can cause human disease. In humans, this fungus causes a red, scaly, circular rash.

2) **Scabies.** Scabies is a skin disease that is caused by a mite. These mites cause intense itching and hair loss in dogs and cats. Humans can pick up the mite by just petting an affected animal. In humans it can cause a red, itchy rash.

3) **Chlamydia.** This disease is caused by a bacteria found primarily in birds (pet birds as well as chickens and ducks). It can cause serious illness in some birds but others may appear healthy and only harbor the infection. These bacteria can be transmitted to humans by inhaling dust from bird feces or feathers. In humans, it can cause a serious, flu-like illness and even death in young children or immuno-compromised people.

4) **Salmonella.** This is a serious bacterial disease in animals that generally causes severe diarrhea and dehydration. Salmonella is commonly transmitted by contact with reptile, amphibian or bird feces. (It is rarely transmitted by contact with dog and cat feces.) In humans, it also causes severe diarrhea and dehydration and in young children or immuno-compromised humans, it can cause death.

5) **Cat Scratch Fever.** This disease is caused by unidentified bacteria. It is transmitted primarily by scratches, licks or bites. In humans, it can cause severe infection including lymph node enlargement, high fever, and flu-like symptoms. Many humans will require hospitilazation.

6) **Lyme Disease, Rocky Mountain Spotted Fever and Erlichiosis.** All three of these bacterial infections are spread by ticks. They cause similar symptoms in humans and animals. Common signs in all species include joint swelling, fever, arthritis and bleeding. Advise clients to keep ticks off of their animals—for their animals' health as well as for their own.

7) **Rabies.** Rabies is a deadly virus transmitted through bite wounds. Make sure all clients' animals have been vaccinated. Report all bites to your local animal control department.

8) **Roundworms.** These are common parasites found in dogs and cats. Humans can become infected through contact with infected animal's feces. In young children and immuno-compromised humans this parasite can cause liver and eye disease. Cases of brain abscesses have also been reported. Always wash your hands after fecal contact!

Unfortunately, I do not have enough room in this column to list all the diseases that can be transmitted to humans from animals. Know the risks involved in handling animals and always seek medical attention for any bites, skin lesions or illness that develops after animal handling. Remember, wash your hands often, especially after handling clients' pets.

Advertising and Marketing
Business Practices
Disaster Planning
Networking

Advertising and Marketing

Advertising and marketing are the main avenues of communication between a pet-sitting business and potential customers. If pet owners do not know a service exists, they cannot become clients. In order for any business to grow and prosper, marketing is a key factor.

From advice on getting news releases published, to the advantages of participating in community events, *The WORLD* has been providing guidance and offering new and innovative marketing ideas to its members.

PSI Takes Stance Against Negative Advertising

Summer 1996 Vol. III, Issue 3

Negative advertising is the practice of tearing down other services in an attempt to build up your own service. Usually, it backfires. In pointing a finger at a problem, three fingers are pointed back, casting aspersion on our entire industry.

The use of negative advertising by pet sitters usually takes aim at three targets—boarding at kennels, boarding at veterinary offices and other pet-sitting services. PSI has taken a stand against the use of negative advertising and does not condone such actions by our members.

We suggest that any PSI member who is using—or is contemplating using—negative advertising, thoroughly think this matter through. Consider changing any negative slant to a more positive, constructive angle.

PSI advocates the use of positive advertising, which promotes the beneficial features of at-home pet care services.

There will always be competition in business. By adhering to the strengths of positive advertising, we will demonstrate responsibility, professionalism and commitment to the high standards set forth in our *Recommended Quality Standards of Excellence in Pet Sitting.*

Marketing Your Business through Local Law Enforcement Agencies

by Belea Keeney, Purrfect Pet Sitter Inc., Pinellas County, FL

Summer 1996 Vol. III, Issue 3

Once you've established your basic marketing strategies as outlined in "*Pet Sitting for Profit*;" i.e., take-one stands, bulletin boards, Yellow Pages, etc., it's time to expand your marketing to other avenues. One good approach to try is making presentations at local Crime Watch, crime prevention and Neighborhood Watch meetings, offered through your local law enforcement agencies.

Most urban area agencies and some smaller, rural departments have Crime Prevention/Crime Watch programs. For big city agencies, they are often a completely separate unit with multiple officers working under a supervisor. Smaller agencies often add Crime Watch to other duties for ranking officers. First, check your local government listings in the phone book and see if they have a specific phone number for their Crime Watch unit. Then it's time to call and see who is in charge of the unit and which officers you should approach about doing presentations/seminars at local meeting.

It helps to understand the basic structure of law enforcement agencies. In general, police departments are operated by city governments and cover a geographic area within certain city limits. Sheriff's departments, on the other hand, are generally operated by county governments and cover an entire county. For example, in Pinellas County, FL, where I live, there is one sheriff's office, but there are 24 different municipalities within the county and each has its own police department! Since sheriff's departments are more spread out, they are less likely to have a formal Crime Watch unit in operation, but check to make sure.

Remember in dealing with law enforcement agencies, that their hierarchy is based on a paramilitary structure; this means that rank is important! Usually, entry level police personnel are referred to as "Officers" and unranked sheriff's personnel are "Deputies." (Highway patrol officers are usually "Troopers.") Their ranks are on their name badges when you meet them in person. When approaching law enforcement personnel, find out their rank and use it in conversation and correspondence. It may be that the Crime Prevention Unit in your area is primarily staffed by civilians; that is, non-sworn personnel. This means they do not carry guns, don't have arrest powers and therefore have no rank. Address them as Mr. or Ms. until they ask you to do otherwise.

Now, depending on whether you prefer to send an introductory letter or to make a cold call, it's time to write up your idea emphasizing the benefits of your business to the officer in charge. You're offering a valuable service that actually helps make your law enforcement agency's job easier! After all, you perform security checks on the homes you're visiting in addition to the pet care you provide. Mention that you have a short presentation prepared and that you'd be glad to do it at future Crime Watch meetings. If you send a letter, you can modify the letter in *"Pet Sitting for Profit"* and add some local information about you and your company. Then, follow up with a polite phone call to see if there is any interest from the Crime Watch Unit. Even if they don't allow speakers at neighborhood meetings, you might suggest that your brochures would be informative to citizens. Always ask. If nothing else, you might get the officer you speak with as a client or at least he or she will be educated about the valuable services you provide and may refer you to citizens.

Now, if you are invited to make a presentation, here are some tips. First, take your cue from the officer in charge with regard to how much time you can take and how much you should talk about pet sitting *per se* versus home security measures. Second, you should make an outline of what topics you'd like to cover. Third, practice at least three times before your speech! Use your family and friends as an audience and get their feedback on where you might improve. Have them ask you questions so you can get used to thinking on your feet and responding well in front of a crowd. Once you've done a few presentations, your routine will be down pat and you'll be much more comfortable doing your "dog and pony show."

Remember that your presentation needs to be concise and spirited. Move around the podium or the front of the room. Use visual aids if available. If you have access to a VCR and some cute video, use that. Display blown up photos of your client's pets or pass around your photo scrapbook. Remember, most people are interested in your job. They'll want to hear about some funny stories; the strange cooking instruction you've carried out and the quirky habits of some of your pet charges. Get them ready to relax and laugh and you'll be relaxed, too. You'll need to make yourself available afterward for the shy people who were too embarrassed to ask questions during your talk.

The law enforcement agency you're working with may not allow you to use your company name during a presentation. If so, just prepare a generic speech about pet sitting services and the security measures they provide to their clients. Some law enforcement agencies frown on anyone passing out brochures or business cards; others are more flexible about it. For example, a Crime Watch meeting I attended had a discussion about anti-car theft devices. The brand names "The Club" and "LoJack" were never mentioned, although a Club was passed around the room. Emphasize the security measures you perform for the traveling client. This should include taking in the mail and newspapers, watering outside plants, opening/closing blinds and curtains, operating alarm systems, adjusting televisions and radios and leaving lights on and off inside and outside the house. If you do house checks for petless clients, mention that as well.

Depending on your Crime Watch officer's advice, you may want to ask people to reconsider canceling their mail and newspaper deliveries. In St. Petersburg last year, we had a series of burglaries at vacationer's homes. It turned out the criminals had gained access to a "stop deliver" list through an employee for the local newspaper. Mail and newspaper personnel with that sort of information can be a source of problems.

In addition to company brochures (if allowed), offer a "How to Select a Pet Sitter" checklist based on Pet Sitters International's Recommended Quality Standards for Excellence in Pet Sitting. Check to see if it's possible to include your company logo without your business name on any handouts; that way people can find you in the phone book if the logo is in the Yellow Pages, too. Add questions to the list that make your company look good. I customized mine with additional questions that showed my company in the best light. For example, since I owned the oldest pet-sitting company in the county, I included a question that made longevity an asset.

I also emphasized that my operation was a full-time venture as opposed to the majority of pet sitters in the area, which were strictly part-time operations. If you're a vet tech, include a question about experience with animals. Emphasize your company's positive traits through the use of clever questions.

If your time is limited, you may want to do meetings in the higher income areas of your region. Obviously these residents are more likely to be your clients than a lower income area. If you don't have a choice, though, be gracious and do all the meetings.

In addition to the pragmatic benefits of Crime Watch, it is also an opportunity to participate in your city. Neighborhood Crime Watches have had a real positive impact on their communities. Plus, you'll meet some interesting, odd, fun and flaky people—your neighbors! The people who have seen your talks will remember you and have a sense that they already "know" you and trust you. Doing Crime Watch presentations helps to promote pet sitting in general. All in all, it's a two-hour investment in time that can really pay off.

Summary

- Find out who handles local Crime Watch and approach.
- Practice a short presentation.
- Prepare a generic checklist to hand out.
- Do an animated presentation and connect with potential clients!

Editor's Note: This is a great marketing idea and instance where having a local PSI Network may make inroads. If your local Crime Watch program is reluctant to promote any "one" pet sitting service, they may be more receptive to working with your local pet-sitting network to promote at-home pet care (and the crime deterrence it provides!) in general.

Expand Your Services – Increase Your Sales!

by Belea T. Keeney

May/June 1997 Vol VI, Issue 3

How would you like to make more money? No, this is not a commercial by Sally Struthers to hawk high school diplomas by mail! It is an "ideafest" to jump-start your business with concepts for service expansion that will increase your gross sales **and** your net profits.

Maybe you feel that your pet-sitting business has maxed out its sales in your marketing area. Maybe you're just itching for a new challenge. Maybe you **need** to generate more money. Whatever your reasons, expanding your services beyond basic pet sitting can help you and your business. It will take some management skills; both your personal time management and the time for employee/subcontractor management and supervision.

The basic concept is to generate more dollars from the clients you have now, more clients and money for new services and to cross-market your services for a profitable synergy. The idea – more $$ for less work and effort and here's how.

You probably have ideas of your own about new pet services you could be offering. Here are some ideas for pet-related services that might fit into your business:

Doggie day care. We already know of the "latchkey" dogs in your customers' lives. Now think about offering them a doggie day care center where they could drop Fido off for canine play group while mom or dad works all day. Wouldn't some of them jump at the chance for Fido to have company, entertainment and some supervision during the day? You can charge fees on a weekly or daily basis and for the ultra-busy pet parent, even offer to pick up and deliver Fido.

Pet taxi service. Provide an animal limousine service for busy or non-driving pet parents. You can take animals to the veterinarian, the groomers, to Aunt Sarah's or wherever they need to go. Set your prices based on distance traveled, time involved, the number of pets you're transporting and the overhead cost of your vehicle.

Overnight service. Client's have probably already asked you about staying overnight in their homes. It gives a home added security and more time and attention for the pets. One drawback in providing this service is finding mature, reliable employees (or subcontractors) who are willing to do it. Base your fees on current market rates and split the fee with your employee.

In-home sitters. This is different from overnight service because you place pets in private homes for sitting. It's like going to Grandma's for vacation! Recruit retirees, stay-at-home parents and work-at-home telecommuters who can care responsibly for pets. Set your fees 20-25 percent higher than area kennels (because pets are getting personalized around-the-clock attention) and split it with your sitter.

Pet grooming. If you're already trained and experienced in grooming, it's an easy transition to provide a mobile grooming service for your clients. Offer bathing, clipping, conditioning and "accessorizing" for pets. Base your fees on what the area competition charges.

Pet training. Again, a sideline service that provides an easy seque into offering pet-sitting services. If you can provide classes for puppy and dog training, you have a built-in clientele for your daily dog-walking services. You can arrange to provide classes in conjunction with a local pet retailer, either on or off site. Or offer private sessions at your client's home.

Aquarium maintenance. If you're experienced and knowledgeable about fresh and saltwater fish tanks, there may be a market for an aquarium maintenance service in your area. Contact local fish supply stores to get a sense of the market and feel them out about providing such a service. (Some stores do it themselves, so don't be put off if they are negative to you at first.) Your clients will need you to provide weekly or monthly cleaning, stocking and water analysis services. Base your fees on the time involved and a markup for any products that you provide.

Retail pet products. You've probably noticed what kinds of pet supplies your clients use. Think about selling the most popular products to your clientele in conjunction with pet food delivery. Set your prices at a reasonable retail price that includes delivery or charge a flat fee for delivery. Either way, it's easier for your clients to have you come in, say, every month, with all their pet supplies than for them to run around town every week or so to stock their pet pantry. This service especially appeals to busy professionals and working couples with limited leisure time.

Pet parties. Offer to do pet holiday and birthday parties for a group of pets (typically dogs). You can provide a special gourmet tuna birthday cake, party hats and favors, doggie games and, of course, photos of the entire event. Have your client generate the guest list and handle the RSVPs and give you an exact count of pet guests. If you get asked to do the human food catering (and you will), you can evade it by saying you're not licensed to provide food for human consumption and send them to the local deli for a party platter. Pet parties can be a lot of fun. Base your fee on the time involved, the cost of food and favors you provide and the number of guests.

Pet photos. With a couple of neutral backdrops, a good quality camera, adequate lighting and a good command of animal behavior, you can take precious photographs of your clients' pets. Offer an in-home studio session that includes a specific number of shots of film (typically 24 or 36 for a single animal), with two or three backgrounds and/or costume changes. You can charge a flat fee for the sitting and then a fee for the photos based on size and number ordered.

Personalized pet gifts. Offer pets' names on any number of items for your clients. Pet placemats, bowls, collars, leashes. Picture frames, treat jars, just about anything and everything associated with pet care can be personalized. Use your imagination here! This can be especially profitable for the holiday season, when people need gifts for their friends and family.

Plan through the logistics of your new service. If you're doing a pet taxi service, for example, you will need to do a pre-trip interview/pet profile for each pet? Do you want to do that just for dogs or for all pets? How much will you charge? Have a plan and policies in place before you offer the service. That way, if Mrs. Fitch calls and wants you to take all eight of her cats to the vet, you'll already know that you'll be charging extra for more than two animals.

Use your current marketing strategies to generate new clients and let your current clients know about your new services(s). Add a section to your brochures or place inserts in them if you feel that you have too many on hand to toss out. Add to your list of services and fees that you send potential clients, put a feature story on your new service in your monthly newsletter and send out postcards with a discounted price for your new service. And seriously consider sending out press releases to area media, particularly if your new service lends itself to being photographed. Animal stories are often in demand for local news shows and local newspapers.

Your new service probably won't cost all that much to get up and running. You already have a business phone and license, a bonding and insurance policy and a business "infrastructure" in place. Your overhead is unlikely to increase significantly. Sit down and figure your expenses and revenues for three months and give it a try. If it doesn't work out, any losses will be minimal.

If one of your add-on services does really take off, your can always morph into a separate business entity and either sell it off completely or have an employee manage the whole operation while you take a cut for overhead, marketing and profit.

Expanding your services can provide additional income and additional clients for you in exchange for providing needed assistance to your pet friends!

How Can You Get Your Pet-Sitting Business Mentioned in the Newspaper?

by Joan S. Rodgers, Piedmont Parent, Greensboro, NC

Sept/Oct 1999 Vol VI, Issue 5

This is the first in a series of articles about how to get media coverage for your pet sitting business.

How can you get your pet-sitting business mentioned in the newspaper? In two words, **call first**.

Otherwise, if you plan a grand opening or publicity stunt, you might be disappointed. Many a ribbon cutting and check presentation has gone uncovered by daily newspapers. On the other hand, a weekly newspaper might routinely cover such events. Before planning an event, speak to an editor and ask if the newspaper will cover your event.

Most papers prefer a story with more substance. A better approach would be to offer some pet-related information that could be the basis of an interesting story. Offer information with which you are familiar. Be specific. If someone from the newspaper interviews you about your area of expertise, your name and profession will be mentioned.

First, call and ask for a features editor. A metro-desk or city-desk editor generally handles "hard" or breaking news. The features department is the place for a human-interest story.

Tell the features editor you have a list of amusing things that you have seen pets do when you were caring for them, or a list of some of the darnedest things that pet owners do. You can describe some of the amusing, harmless quirks of pet owners without naming names. For example, you might say: "One woman has to sing 'Your Cheatin' Heart' to get her collie to tolerate his bath, and a man has taught his mynah bird to cheer for his favorite football team." Editors and readers will no doubt find such behavior endearing.

These examples might lead to a discussion about what pet sitters do, which could be the subject of a story. You might want to mention Pet Sitters International and have PSI's phone number handy [(336) 983-9222] if the editor wants information on a national level. This will lend you credibility, and you can provide the local pet angle.

Another angle is simply to call and let the editor know you operate a pet-sitting business and would be happy to serve as a source about pets. Give seasonal examples: "For hurricane season, I could give you some tips about preparing for a pet's care during a disaster. During hot weather, I can point out some precautions owners can take for pets that stay outdoors. Or, at vacation time, I could explain what a pet sitter does. For the holidays, I could give you some gift ideas for the household dog or cat."

Spin story ideas off pop culture. Editors love to localize national news. When the president gets a new dog and wonders what to name it, that's a good time to call the editor, mention the president's dog and offer the year's 10 most popular pet names. When a new movie about a dog or cat comes out, that's a good time to propose a pet story. Find a way to tie a story to the movie and point out the connection to the editor. If the main character is a St. Bernard, propose a story about the facts and lore about St. Bernard's. Provide the editor with the facts and lore, and be ready with the name and phone number of a local St. Bernard you know--and its owner (a client). Check with the owner first and make sure he's willing to be interviewed.

Let the editor know your professional relationship with the St. Bernard's owner and (to get yourself mentioned in the story) offer your own affectionate observations about Bruiser, with the owner's approval. Time your proposal a few weeks in advance of the movie's release, if possible, so the story can coincide with the opening of the movie. Some feature pages are planned weeks in advance.

You might propose a local story about businesses that plan to participate in *Take Your Dog To Work Day*®. Offer names of employees and employers, with their permission, who plan to participate. Call PSI for more information to offer the editor (and to get pet sitting mentioned in the story).

Another approach is to call the newspaper and ask for the business editor. Many business desks run stories about new or unusual businesses. Since much of the public has yet to be educated about pet sitting, the industry might strike the business editor as a cutting-edge topic.

Some people badger, insult or shame editors to try to get them to run a story. This is not the best approach. More than likely, editors will be objective and judge the story on its merits, but they're only human. If you alienate them, they may not go out of their way to give you some of their space in print. You don't want to become one of those rare people whom everyone at the newspaper avoids. It's also not a good idea to tell editors that you need publicity. This is a turn-off. It isn't their job to give free publicity to organizations and businesses. Their job is to find and run stories that they believe will interest and inform the reader. Editors and reporters always have the reader in mind. Flattery won't get you far. Editors have heard it all. Paying for ads in the newspaper doesn't carry any weight for a story. Editors make their decisions based on news value. Focusing on rich content is your best bet.

A photo may help. Today, newspapers are "art-driven." An editor might be on the fence about running a story, but the offer of a good-quality photo could make a difference. It could save the publication the effort and expense of sending a photographer to shoot a photo to run with the story.

If your business can afford it, have a professional photo made that will illustrate your message. It will be worth the cost. Have a photo made of yourself with your own pet in a beautiful setting. Or have a photo made of an appealing pet you know, a handsome malamute, frolicking black Lab puppies, a regal Siamese or a dog taking care of a cat.

If you can't afford a professional photographer, shoot a photo yourself. A common mistake is not getting close enough to the subject. Get within four or five feet. If outdoors, stand with the sun behind you and, to avoid hard shadows, don't shoot around noon. Remember not to photograph the back of someone's head. It makes for an uninteresting shot. Think about composition. Have a focal point. Don't have a big empty spot in the center of the photo. Candid shots are more interesting than still shots, though a good quality portrait of a pet with its human goes a long way.

If you feel that you would make a better impression in writing than on the telephone, write a press release or announcement. There's no need to spend a great deal of time and money to give it an extra-attractive presentation. Editors and reporters want substance. They're not impressed if a press release has been placed inside an expensive folder or has a free gift attached. They like to have something in writing to hand back and forth and to remind them about the information. It doesn't have to be in any particular form or beautifully written. They will use it as background. It does need to contain good ideas. Just write up some ideas, similar to those given above. Put the most important information first and be brief. Try to confine it to one page.

Call the newspaper and ask a receptionist or clerk the name and work address, or fax number, of a specific features or business editor and mail or fax the release to that person. Don't send your ideas by e-mail unless you have spoken to the editor and it has been requested. It could get lost among hundreds of e-mail messages from readers firing off letters and suggestions:

Include a business card and a brochure, if your business has one. One or two weeks later, follow up with a phone call and make yourself available if anyone is interested, but don't be pushy. If the editor isn't interested, offer to be an available source for comments about pet care. (Take care to defer to veterinarians about medical care.)

Calling another editor at the same newspaper is usually not wise. Editors are pretty reliable when it comes to passing an idea to another department if they can't use it themselves. It's somewhat frustrating for one to handle something only to find it coming in again through another editor. If you want to try again at the same newspaper, ask the first editor what he thinks. You might ask him about "zoned" sections that serve smaller communities in a daily's circulation area and about special sections on the marketing side, which operates separately from the news-editorial side.

If you like to write, you might consider writing a piece yourself. Most daily newspapers won't be interested in a self-written article. What they might be interested in is a guest column for the opinion-editorial, or "op-ed" page. Read the newspaper closely for a few weeks to see if it runs guest pieces. Call the editorial-page department and ask for guidelines, including the number of words you're allowed to write. Then create a thoughtful and well-crafted essay about a timely pet-related issue. Include your name, phone-number and the name of your pet-sitting business. A weekly newspaper or a neighborhood/shopping-center newsletter might welcome your story ideas. Some of these publications may let you write the story yourself. You still need an angle. Write a cohesive piece that "hangs together."

If your business has its own newsletter, consider putting the local newspaper's features and business editors on your mailing list. They may get a story idea from it sometime. You'll want to think of new angles **all** the time for your newsletter. If you employ other pet sitters, ask them for ideas. And ask your clients what kind of articles they would like to read. Remember, content rules.

Talking to Editors

What **not** to say:

- You're always running bad news. Do you want some good news?

- I really need this publicity to help my business.

- If you run an article, I can use it in a brochure to show clients.

- You should run my story because I buy ads in your newspaper.

What to say:

- In my work, I have collected some charming anecdotes about pets. I think they could be the basis of a great story.

- Are you familiar with the pet-sitting profession?

- Would you like to know the top 10 pet names this year?

- Perhaps you will keep me in mind if you need comments about pet care and related issues.

I'm a Gorilla, and You Can Be a Gorilla, Too!

by Lani Stites, The Hum Cat Lady, Bangor, ME

July/Aug 1999 Vol VI, Issue 4

"Hello, my name is Lani and I'm a pet sitter, and I'm a gorilla." This is my new mantra after attending a workshop here in my hometown with Jay Conrad Levinson, the author of over a dozen books on Guerrilla Marketing. At first I was surprised that such an international speaker would travel to our remote area of Northern California, almost on the Oregon border. But, Levinson lives only about six hours south, in Marin County, just north of the Golden Gate Bridge. He certainly dressed the part–all those clichés are true–deck shoes, no socks, Levis under a sports jacket and opened collar shirt. I had to remind myself that this is the man who created Marlboro Country and many more advertising successes along the way. He even says he is now sometimes ashamed to admit he created the Marlboro Man.

For three hours, Levinson stood before us with no notes, no charts or overheads, and he talked as fast as I've ever heard any man talk before. I was mesmerized. Even more importantly, I was delighted to hear his 100 points of Guerrilla Marketing. As he put it, when you hear some of these ideas a red asterisk will go off in your head - you know that this idea will work for your company.

Here are 10 of his ideas that I've already put to work:

1. **Gorillas Provide Client Care and Feeding.** Showing that you care about your clients is the #1 marketing technique and the easiest to do. For example, I recently attended a local light opera production of the "Sound of Music." When one of the main characters came on stage I saw that it was one of my cat clients. The next day I sent her a note telling her how good the show was and how lucky Oliver (the cat) is to have such a talented 'mom.' Another client has trouble with her eyesight. I never asked about why her eyesight was so poor. Then one Sunday in the newspaper there was an article about a book she had published on her recovery from a major head injury and how her cats and new puppy helped her recover. My note to her congratulated her on being an author and expressed delight that her pets were bringing her this comfort.

2. **Gorillas Open Their Mouths and Ask Questions.** "All you gotta do is ask." Ask each client to give you names/addresses of three or four pet-owning friends within your service area. Leave a blank piece of paper and a SASE so they can fill it out at their leisure. They will be sure to mail it since it has a stamp. All you have to do is follow up with a newsletter or introductory letter to the new names.

3. **Even the Zoo Has Hours Posted.** All in-home businesses should have hours and days of operation. Even if it's a two-hour block from 6 a.m.—8 a.m. on Sunday mornings, announce the hours on your answering machine and literature. Some people still detest answering machines and will call back when they know you're available.

4. **Gorillas Bribe with Food** (or anything else you can think of). Levinson says to give bribes shamelessly, even if it's just a small/low-priced item. Last Christmas I bought large tins of popcorn for about $3 each. I put a name tag on it, addressing it "To The Staff". I took one can to each vet office and you should have seen the surprised faces of the staff when I told them it was for them to share, not for the vet to take home. I have worked in offices where the boss got all the gifts and it wasn't much fun. Make friends with the "gatekeepers" and you'll always find the door open.

5. **Gorillas Don't Eat Yellow Pages.** No, the Yellow Pages are not for every business and part of guerrilla marketing is knowing how to spend advertising dollars. However, Levinson says if you are in the Yellow Pages, never tell the client to look you up in there. After all, they will be looking at a page full of competitors' ads. If you are stuck in a situation with no business cards you should say "Look me up in the business section of the white pages." Levinson also says do **not** spell out something cute with your phone number - it's too confusing to clients. (I think there may be two sides to this theory.)

6. **FREE Admission for Gorillas Only.** Smile often, make eye contact and use the name of the pet. These are absolutely free ways to market your sincerity to the client. Your telephone demeanor is free too. Sometimes it's hard to be pleasant when you just spent 12 hours pet sitting, but the caller doesn't know that and can't see your body language - they'll just think you are cranky. Enthusiasm and passion are free tools. Every pet sitter I've met at the PSI conventions has oozed passion for this business. Use it to sell yourself and your service to customers. It's worth more than degrees or titles behind your name. Levinson says 70 percent of business is lost due to apathy. Don't let this happen to you.

7. **Follow-up Care and Feeding from the Gorilla.** Follow-up is always important, but consider sending different brochures for different situations:
   - **New clients** who just used you have a 30-day 'satisfaction period.' Follow-up with a letter that will prolong that satisfied feeling.
   - **Prospective clients** who called and asked for a free brochure should get specialized information so they will feel good about calling you again.
   - **Regular clients** who want to give your info to others require a different type of hand-out (a discount for referral maybe?).

Another technique: Use catchy envelopes or stamps that will grab attention and get opened. If you can afford it, have your logo printed on envelopes. Levinson says to put 33 individual 1 cent stamps, but I think this may be too tedious! I have a pattern for making envelopes out of calendar pages and posters which I use as an attention-getter. When creating your brochure or literature consider "Know where to hang your hat." Find what you do that others don't and emphasize that. Make your business card an educational tool as well.

8. **It Takes a Village to Raise a Gorilla.** Community involvement will set you apart from strangers. When I first started my business I was not the only pet sitter in our small town. But, I was the only pet sitter to join the county Humane Society. I'm still the only pet sitter to donate gift certificates to the biannual auction for public television. It's for a good cause and the goodwill is priceless.

9. **Gorillas Can Educate and Train.** Guerrilla Marketing urges small business owners to speak to local service organizations. Use the knowledge you have in your special field to educate and entertain others. Most organizations, like Women in Business and the Lion's Club, are desperate for fresh new speakers. The idea is to speak on a subject you know something about, not to stand up and advertise your business. Go to Toastmasters to learn public speaking. My speech, "Everything you always wanted to know about cats," went out in letters to clubs in the area so they could consider adding me to their speaking calendar. The speech is fun history, trivia and cat lore, but of course, I will have my pet-sitting name tag on and will take business cards and brochures.

10. **Gorillas: Toot Your Own Horn.** According to Levinson, if you get a write-up in the newspaper you should exploit it for at least 10 years! You should mount the article, laminate it, frame it, take it to initial interviews, send copies of it with your brochures, etc. The same is true if your company wins an award. If you don't toot your own horn, nobody else will – so TOOT, TOOT!

I own a small pet-sitting company and many of the Guerilla Marketing ideas don't apply to me. Some of them I was already doing (pat on the back). However, I am always open to new ways to promote my business as I hope you are too. Jay Levinson ended his workshop with the question: "When is the best time to plant a tree?" His answer was "Either 20 years ago or tomorrow." Then he asked, "When should you start guerrilla marketing?" - same answer, 20 years ago or tomorrow.

> **"Sometimes when you hear an idea, a red asterisk will go off in your head, and you know that this idea will work for your company."**
>
> *-Jay Conrad Levinson*

Low Budget/High Energy Advertising: Hold a Pet Care Fair Day!

by Liz SanSebastian, Pet Companions

February 1995 Vol. II, Issue 1

Two months after starting my pet sitting service I evaluated my phone interview surveys, under the section of "How Did You Learn About Our Company?" I found that 80 percent of my clients had learned about us from business cards I had posted at a local pet store. I realized this pet store was a good point of sale for my business, which led me to think about what else I could do at this location to further increase sales.

As a long time pet lover, I was always looking for animal-related functions I could attend to learn about pet care and new pet products. This gave me the idea to organize a "Pet Care Fair Day" where I could meet with pet owners and tell them about my services. I could contact other pet care-related businesses and ask them if they would like to set up information booths at this event to make the public aware of their services and meet potential clients face-to-face.

The next day I went to the pet store and spoke to the manager. He said we could hold the event in their parking lot and place fliers around the store. I gathered the names of several pet care-related businesses in the area which included dog training services, a pet tattooing company, a local kennel, a mobile grooming company, a company that painted pet portraits, and another pet-sitting service. Five companies agreed to participate in the event.

We all agreed on a date in early fall that corresponded with the pet store's fall sale—something sure—to maximize public turnout!

When the day arrived for the "Pet Care Fair Day," the weather was great and the pet owners were happy to meet and talk with all of us. Each participant had a table with a sign bearing the company's name and logo and was staffed with a representative who could discuss services with pet owners. The kennel had a free drawing for a pet gift basket; the dog training company gave demonstrations of dog obedience; the pet tattooing company had their tattooing equipment out for the public to see and touch; the pet portrait company had examples of their art work (with the actual dogs sitting next to them) and I gave away key chains, with my company name and phone number, and gift certificates for free pet-sitting visits.

We estimated that approximately 50 people passed through each of our booths, and I have picked up five new clients, to date. We all agreed it was a success and plan on holding the event again in the spring. The pet store was happy with the event and offered us free advertising in their newsletter for our next event. The five exhibiting companies have agreed to pool advertising money and take out a one-page ad in the local paper announcing the spring Pet Care Fair Day.

I met a lot of great people, pet owners and business people alike through the event that I otherwise may not have had the opportunity to work with. I highly recommend that other pet-sitting services hold a similar type of "fair" to increase their business!

Liz SanSebastion at her first annual Pet Care Fair Day

Most pet sitters admit that they absolutely detest paperwork and would rather be out caring for pets. But to ensure long-term success, a pet sitter must be an astute business person, too. And that means scheduling, installing office procedures, client billing and communications, and even staffing, legal and licensing issues.

To provide this information to PSI members, *The WORLD* taps a number of helpful resources that have included PSI staff members, educators, outside experts and experienced pet sitters who have generously shared their experiences with their colleagues.

Business Practices

Holiday Traffic
Finding Time for Yourself

by Clarice J. Pugh, Whiskers, Wings and Other Things LLC,

Kingston Springs, TN

Nov/Dec 1999, Vol. VI, Issue 6

"Hi, I heard your message and know you're filled up, but we just got a call from my husband's mother, and his brother is able to come home for Christmas this year. He's stationed in Korea and this is the first time the family's been together for over four years. Please, can't you squeeze us in? All you have to do is give Fluffy fresh food and water. We know you're busy; you don't have to spend any time with Fluffy. Please, we're desperate..."

I'll bet every pet sitter in the world receives a call like this at least once every holiday. Something totally unexpected comes up and a great client needs your help. At a recent meeting of several pet sitters, there was a moment of silence when the question was asked, "How long has it been since any of you enjoyed a holiday'?" The silence was followed by several nervous giggles and a few "not since we've been pet sitting" exclamations.

It may be helpful, as the holidays approach, to consider the following:

1) Every day has just 24 hours. How many hours do you need to sleep in order to work efficiently, drive safely, guard your own health and keep your normally sweet disposition when a family member says, "Good morning?"

2) When do you celebrate the "big family meal" during the day, and how much time do you need to spend with everyone before you head out the door to cover more calls? Would it be possible to change the family meal just a little bit?

3) You absolutely need to figure in at least an hour sometime during the day when you can sit down and rest, have a cup of tea and share the excitement of new toys with the kids. This hour can mean the difference between a peaceful holiday versus one of total burnout and stress.

4) Add 1, 2, & 3 together. Now, estimate travel time (usually 15-20 minutes travel time per client). Subtract the total of all of the above

from 24 hours. That's approximately how much time during the day you have to make visits.

For the sake of argument, let's say you can work very well with five hours of sleep, plus two hours for the family dinner and one hour for "R&R." That totals eight hours. Let's also say you've figured out travel time to and from client homes will take two hours and forty minutes. You end up with thirteen hours and ten minutes for pet sitting. You know you can at least handle thirteen calls.

Additional calls you can reasonably fit in will be determined by:

A) How well you've scheduled your route to move from client to client without backtracking.

B) If there are any animals on medication which require you to be at a home at a specific time.

C) Calls that have several animals and will automatically take longer.

D) How much help you can expect from your staff or family. (If you do plan on using a spouse, older child or reliable friend to assist you on holiday calls, make certain you clear this in advance with your client.)

You can run into unexpected situations such as several "accidents" to clean up or an animal that seems to be sick. The extra-time scenarios can cut heavily into your schedule. It may be helpful for you to "imagine" one or two spaces in your schedule as filled. Then, should an emergency such as illness, child birth or a family death occur, you'll be in the position to take that assignment.

Should you end up not needing the time, enjoy the break!

Make every effort to plan your own tasks as far in advance as possible. Wrap presents as you buy them. Bake and freeze holiday treats early in November. Start getting holiday cards and newsletters ready to mail in October. Start getting ready for holiday assignments in June. Advertise holiday scheduling in your summer newsletter. Put messages on your machine indicating that early bookings are required. Learn to say, "No" when you reach the cut-off point you know you can live with. You have the right and obligation to your family and pets under your care to stop. *Remember that one of the main values of in-home pet care is that animals are getting quality time and attention. Remind late callers that it is your policy to ensure that every animal receives the love they need and deserve.*

One additional note: For really busy holidays, I make a list of client names, a space to check off visits, a space to check off when they've made their "We're back home" call, and a line showing the total amount due.

It gives me a warm feeling to know that my clients are able to enjoy a special time away, knowing that their pets are getting love, attention and excellent care. It's nice to know that a friendly meow or wagging tail is waiting to greet you. The time spent driving between assignments is a great opportunity to reflect on your own blessings and to review all of the wonderful lessons you've learned from this unique experience. And, finally, you know you are not alone. There are more than three thousand other pet sitters out there, many of them handling the calls alone, and they understand you!

God bless you and Merry Christmas!

Licensed: What Does it Mean?

February 1996, Vol. III, Issue 1

We continue to see the word "licensed" on pet sitter's business cards and promotional literature. However, we can't understand why this term is being used in our industry.

To date, there isn't any formal "licensing" required to be a professional pet sitter. Electricians have to be licensed in each state, hairdressers have to be licensed, real estate agents are licensed...but where is a licensing program for pet sitters?

The only explanation we can come up with as to why pet sitters are using this term is because they have obtained the proper city, county and/or state privilege license required to operate a business. But so have a myriad of other community businesses. Do they advertise as "licensed?" Obtaining a required business license is, simply put, a cost of doing business. A business license means nothing as to how qualified you are as a professional pet sitter.

We are concerned that the use of this term on advertising materials is misleading to the general public and would like to encourage PSI members to discontinue the practice as the need arises to reprint your business cards and literature. Pet sitting is a profession that is very dependent upon old-fashioned honesty, trustworthiness and integrity. Let's let these traits guide us in the representation of our pet-sitting businesses to the public.

Just Say No!

by Patti Moran

August 1994, Vol. 1, Issue 2

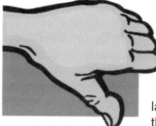

One little word. How can it be so hard to say? Is it something peculiar to the pet-sitting profession that makes saying "no" an impossible feat?

Are we so afraid if we don't accept every last minute reservation or sit for the client with the nasty, filthy home that our business will be doomed for failure? Is it because we're a female-dominated industry or because we're just plain 'ole nice folks in this line of work that "no" doesn't seem to belong in our vocabulary?

Whatever the cause, it's time we realize this is an industry-wide problem all pet sitters face and we must come to terms with it. Our business success and sanity rely heavily upon being able to say, simply and confidently, "no."

We are all guilty of it. You're completely booked for the weekend or maybe you even blocked the weekend out for some much-needed time off. About 9 p.m. on Friday evening the phone rings with a customer begging you for services. You sigh and accept the job even though it will really stretch you or mean giving up the "time off" you'd planned and you'll hate yourself for not saying no!

Or maybe a customer complains about your prices being too high and tries to get you to come down on your fees. Well, you hem and haw, as you sometimes feel guilty charging for fun "easy" jobs, and this is a beautiful home to visit and maybe you could knock a little off your fee.

Or perhaps the client acknowledged on the phone that his/her dog was territorial and had been known to be aggressive towards strangers, but if you're "supposedly a pet care expert, you won't have any problem." So, you agree to set up an initial meeting and dread the situation already.

Or, you know the client's address is in a less than desirable neighborhood where you're not comfortable, yet you hate to turn away business. If there's one thing I've learned in my eleven years in this business, it's to listen to my gut, my instinct, that inner voice, the little radar, and *just say no!*

Think about it. One of the benefits of owning your own business is that you have the power and the right to say "no." You are your own boss and you dictate when, how and for whom you work. Just because you serve the public doesn't mean you have to serve all the people all the time. Just as everyone doesn't shop at Sears, pet-sitting services are not suitable for all occasions (i.e., aggressive dogs, filthy homes). And even Sears closes their door occasionally! They have hours when you can visit or call the store and hours when they are closed.

We pet sitters need to stop "selling ourselves short" and demand to be treated as the respectable business people that we are!

So, how do you begin saying "no?" Here are some suggestions for how to go about it in a tactful manner.

The last minute caller: Deter these calls by adding a "last minute" reservation surcharge to your fees. If you're going to accommodate these inconvenient and sometimes inconsiderate customers, make it worth your time! Besides, when you hit the customer in the pocketbook, they often "get the message."

Another suggestion, especially if your office is in your home, is to establish certain office hours for calls and reservations and then stick to them!

If 1-4 p.m. are your established office hours, then turn the ringer down on your telephone and the sound down on your answering machine at 4 p.m. each day. If you accept calls at all hours of the day and night, people will call you at all hours! However, if you set specific times to take and return calls and then announce these to your customers, they will soon adjust to them! You must set parameters for yourself or you will find burnout looming on the horizon.

Another option for the last minute caller is to just say no! When you explain in a nice tone that you are sorry, you wish you could help them, but that you are totally booked for the weekend—period—they will learn that you are an exclusive service, and if they want to be a part of it, they will need to call you sooner. Saying no can earn additional respect if your caller sees how "in demand" you are!

The client who tries to get you to come down on your fees: Just politely explain that you are a professional pet sitter and, as such, there is more than meets the eye to your services.

There are the "hidden" costs of insurance, bonding, advertising, office overhead, taxes, printing, supplies, gas, etc., that the client can tend to overlook since all he/she is "seeing" is the visit to the home. Once you stand your ground and firmly but tactfully explain this, the client should respect your price setting.

If they don't, then remember our services are not for everyone! As sure as you give a price break, the job will turn out to be the job from hell. Sure, some assignments are "easier" than others, but for every easy assignment there are two more where the fee should be doubled.

The client with the aggressive dog: It's very easy to explain this policy. "Our company policy prohibits us from sitting for pets that have bitten anyone or acted aggressively in the past. I'll be happy to give you some names and phone numbers of kennels in the area or you may want to ask a family member who is familiar with your dog to provide care. I'm sorry we can't help you, but thank you for calling."

The client in the crime-ridden neighborhood: Just simply explain that you don't provide sitting services in that zip code area (or the western part of town or whatever). Explain that you haven't received enough interest in services from that neighborhood to make it worth your while to expand your sitting territory into the area.

You could even offer to take the client's name and number saying that if you start a service route in their neighborhood, you will let them know. Remember, it's your choice where you pet sit and this is a diplomatic way of saying "no!"

The client with the nasty, filthy house: This can be a little more awkward because normally you won't know the condition of the home until you're actually there for the initial interview. If you are uncomfortable with the assignment after seeing the interior of the home, you could simply explain that you just don't feel comfortable in accepting the assignment, and you would prefer that the customer make other arrangements for pet care.

Or, if you're not brave enough to say "no" while face-to-face with the client, call them immediately upon leaving to explain that you have given it some thought while driving home, and you think it would be better if they made alternate arrangements for pet care as you don't feel comfortable with the living/working conditions of the home. Then, promptly return the house key, if you accepted one at the initial interview.

Sure, the client may be angry or upset at this personal criticism of their housekeeping, but better to do that than suffer through a miserable pet-sitting assignment! We can't please everyone, and the sooner we learn this, the smarter we'll be.

The client who requests extra services, late night visits or something above and beyond your typical services: Explaining that lawn mowing or house cleaning is not part of your business should suffice, (you can't blame a person for asking!) however, a referral to these types of services will likely be appreciated by the client.

Or, if you are willing to make an exception and mow the yard or run an errand for the customer, again, make it worth your time! My experience has shown that customers are so glad that you're willing to accommodate their special needs that they will gladly pay your asking price.

The client who criticizes your services and refuses to pay: If you pet sit long enough, you're bound to run into this customer eventually. Regardless of the lengths you went to during the assignment, they are bound and determined that you are at fault and they shouldn't have to pay.

A personal note here: I consider myself to be among the most honest, ethical and fair people around. If I am at fault or think my staff is, in some respect, I will freely admit it and attempt to make amends with the client. However, if I think that my pet sitter or I did everything humanly possible to properly fulfill our contract with the client, then I will fight to the bitter end! In other words, I say "no," we won't take or accept your complaints and allegations, and we expect our bill to be paid. I stand by that even if it means going to Small Claims Court to collect payment.

There are some people and businesses who adhere to the philosophy that the "customer is always right." I have learned that this is not always the case in pet sitting. The customer has the right to have an opinion or to try and get out of paying their bill, but that doesn't make them right!

The important thing to remember is that it is okay to say "no". Standing up for ourselves and our established business policies and practices will only create respect and solidify the professionalism we're commanding for our industry. It will also help you to build confidence in yourself and your abilities - plus, it will preserve your sanity and keep pet sitting a career you enjoy!

How To Build a Newsletter

by Cara L. Haynes, PSI

Jan/Feb 1999, Vol. IV, Issue 1

For those fortunate enough to have attended the newsletter workshop at *Quest*, this review reinforces the highlights. For those who were unable to attend, we would like to share a little of what was covered.

Lani Stites, the workshop presenter, asserts, "A newsletter is a very, very important business tool. You are really missing the boat if you don't get one out to your clients." A newsletter serves as a way to advertise and communicate with clients or potential clients. Lani reinforces, "They build authenticity and reputation as a professional." As Patti Moran stated in *Pet Sitting for Profit,* "Your newsletter provides a service of useful information to your clients and lends credibility and sincerity to the business."

Along with providing beneficial information on pet care, helpful tips and interesting animal facts, a newsletter should also be a means of communicating to your clients information you want them to know. Inform them of specials your business is offering. Provide insight as to any training or classes on animal care you've taken. Basically, use the newsletter to "talk" to clients.

Lani teaches that an effective newsletter should contain about 75 percent educational materials and about 25 percent selling materials – selling your service. Educational material can consist of anything relevant, such as: animal health care, emotional health, exercise for pets, or even great pet stories. You may also want to include select topics that revolve around seasonal events. For instance, for President's Day Lani wrote about past presidential pets. Consider having a client feedback section or even a client profile. Comics or funny stories make good sideline articles.

A general rule of thumb for any newsletter is to use the same layout and logo in every issue to breed familiarity. Always include a table of contents. A standard editorial column from you, the owner, is a good idea also. Typically, a newsletter is at least four pages long (2 back and front 8 ½" x 11" pages). They can be printed annually, semi-annually, quarterly, monthly or as often as you desire. At least one article should be about pet sitting – what to look for in a sitter, credentials, employees, and so on. Lani remarks, "I've found that clients are really looking for an expert who can pass on useful information."

Fulfill these wishes by having a health column and a book or product review column. Really, anything you wish to include goes! One word of caution, be careful to omit controversial topics which could alienate clients. Also, consider that a newsletter doesn't need a lot of fluff. Keep it simple so that readers don't tire quickly. Lani recommends lots of white spaces around columns and simple black and white graphics to keep the letter refreshing.

Information can come from anywhere. There are tons of magazines and books full of information on pets. Pet owners are great sources of pet care tips. The internet is an endless source of trivia and other information. Be careful to avoid plagiarism. You can always write to the editor requesting permission to reprint an article. If you do use paraphrased information, be sure to cite the source. Again, obtaining permission from the author is the safest route. Utilizing copyright-free graphics or materials helps save on cost and time. Lani Stites runs a service which offers camera ready newsletters or fillers for pet sitters who don't have the time to research and prepare their own.

Costs of producing a newsletter can be offset in various ways. For one thing, you can sell advertising space. For those of you without computers, scotch tape and whiteout does wonders. Simply arrange articles and tape them on blank sheets of paper. The quality of copying is now so good that tape lines are invisible when photocopied. Copy the newsletter yourself at a local copy store. By bringing your own paper, you can save even more! If you mail vast quantities, consider getting a bulk mail permit and stamp through your local post office. Hand out newsletters or have them for "free-taking" at a local pet store or veterinarian office. "I've found vets to be much more receptive to a free newsletter in their office than to business cards or brochures," Lani states. Most importantly, get them out there to past clients to jog their memory and let them know you are still thinking about them.

Should You Offer Overnight Pet Sitting?

by Donna K. Lindsey

May/June 1999, Vol. IV, Issue 3

Overnight sitting can be a challenge. Though many of the principles are the same as per-visit sitting, overnights add different aspects that must be considered. The biggest question to consider is if staying overnight at one client's home will interfere with other sitting assignments. This can be determined on an individual basis, but consider a few things before accepting that first assignment:

- Decide before booking what is the longest assignment you will accept.
- Will it be a hardship on your family for you to be away from home?
- Will your pets at home suffer from your absence?
- Keep in mind that you can only service one overnight client at a time instead of several.
- Are the fees you will be able to charge worth the time spent? As with all pet sitting, consider your area of service. If you take on a client in an outlying area and also have visits scheduled in town, you may lose more than you gain.
- Remember that respect for the client's home is of utmost importance. It can be easy to forget that you are working when you are at the client's home on a long term basis.

After considering all angles and deciding you would like to proceed with taking on overnight clients, choose your clients carefully. When a client calls to request an overnight stay, I always consider the following questions:

- How long will the clients be gone? I won't accept assignments longer than two weeks.
- What are the client's expectations regarding time spent at their home? Do they expect you to be there twenty-four hours a day? If so, that could interfere with serving other clients. Let me give you an example. I had one client who wanted me at her home constantly. I felt this was unreasonable considering that this client worked twelve-hour days with no one at home. Also, her dogs had a dog door to go in and out as they pleased. I gently discussed this with the client, and we were able to compromise.

Let me also give you an example of a situation in which I felt it imperative that I not leave the client's home. I had a long-time client who owned an elderly Cairn Terrier. The client called me needing to schedule my services while she went on a business trip, but she was concerned because Toto wasn't doing well. I not only stayed with Toto twenty-four hours, seven days a week, but I slept on the couch because she could no longer go upstairs to the bedrooms. This client's request for my exclusive attention was very reasonable. Toto passed away the following week. I was glad that I was able to offer her some comfort in her final days.

Other Tips:
- If you have client visits at the same time someone requests you to stay at their home, discuss it with the client that wants you to stay overnight. Most clients understand if you need to be gone for a few hours. Most people work and are not home all day.
- If you have any commitments that may take more than a few hours of your time, make sure to discuss them with your prospective client also. It is not fair to charge a client for more time than you will be spending at their home.
- Because family is a top priority, and they put up with enough nonsense supporting us in this sometimes crazy occupation, NEVER schedule overnight sitting on holidays. I don't book overnight jobs the week before or after a holiday either.

Keeping these common sense thoughts in mind should help you make the choice whether or not overnight sitting is best for you.

Planning the Unthinkable

By William S Foster, PSI

August 1995, Vol II Issue 3

The customer was hesitant, her voice apologetic as she spoke. "I hate to mention this, but my husband and I were talking last night. What happens, God forbid, if you and your wife are killed in a car wreck while we are gone? Do you have someone else to care for my pets?"

I had only been in business eight months. Dying was the furthest thing from my mind. The woman had a valid point. What would happen? Nobody but my wife and myself knew the daily call schedule. Nobody knew where the keys were kept or how each key was coded. Nobody knew where the customer history on each pet was kept. What in the world would happen?

I needed to respond to this woman prior to her departure. I developed a "disaster plan" that week which stayed in effect until I sold my business. I expanded my disaster plans to include natural disasters too. Whether you're a one-person pet sitting service or a company with a staff of forty pet sitters, it is wise to develop a disaster plan. Here are some ideas:

1. Death or Disability

In the event of your or your spouse's death, there should be someone who is familiar with your business and who can immediately step in to handle the daily duties of your business. A friend, relative, neighbor, or in our case, a competitor! Think about it. Who better to succeed you if death occurs, than someone already in the business? In our case, it was reciprocal because the firm we chose was independently owned and operated by a sole pet sitter who also happened to be single. If something should happen to her, she had no one to rely on to see that her rounds were made or to care for her business. So, we signed a simple agreement. It stated that in the event of death or disabling injury, we would continue to run the other's business until permanent arrangements could be made. We did not attempt to work out compensation, liability, etc. It was only an agreement to assure each other that our businesses would be protected and our customers' needs would be met.

Both my competitor and I used this contract as a sales tool during future presentations to new customers. It gave each of our clients additional peace of mind.

2. Natural Disaster

What about an earthquake, tornado, hurricane, flood or blizzard? Regardless of your physical location, there is always some natural phenomenon that may occur, disrupting your normal routine. You need a plan that is specific, written and available to your customers so that they will know what to expect from your service should a disaster occur while their pets are under your care. Remember, you are writing this plan ONLY for those customers whose pets are in your charge at the time of the event. We had many requests for in-town customers to "assist them" too in the event of a disaster. We politely declined and explained that we had too much to do for our out-of-town customers!

Here are some points your written policy should contain:

A. Telephone Contact

Check with your local telephone company for their policy. In Southern California (where my pet-sitting service was located), it is useless for a person in New York to attempt to call California. Incoming lines are blocked, allowing people in California to call out-of-state. Your local telephone company procedures should become your telephone policy. In our case, we telephoned each customer where they were located within four hours of the event (earthquake in Southern California!) to advise them of the status of their property and the condition of their pets.

B. Pet Policy

We told our clients that if their pet(s) needed to be moved for safety reasons, we would take those pets to the closest "safe house" for lodging. (We polled our customers and found many with extra carrying cages, kennels, etc., who would be willing to take in pets in an emergency. We had a list of 15 customers in our geographic service area who volunteered to help if conditions permitted.)

C. Future Action

What happens after you move the pets? We told our customers two things:
 a. After we secured the pets (by a move or in their own home), we would call the customer and tell them where and how the pets were doing.
 b. Last, we asked the customer to attempt to get home within three days to personally handle the situation.

The best news is that we never had to totally activate our disaster plan in the seven years we owned the business. We had only minor earthquakes which resulted in our checking in-service customer homes for pet safety and structural damage.

I hope you never have to utilize your disaster plan either. But I can tell you from personal experience that you and your customers will sleep better at night just knowing you have a written disaster plan in place!

Your Pricing is Your Business

by Bill Foster

Jan/Feb 1999, Vol. VI, Issue 1

Have you had the experience of being bluntly asked by a customer, "How did you arrive at the prices you charge for pet sitting?" The question hits you like a cold bucket of water in your face. The first time I was asked this question I stammered, stumbled and finally mumbled an excuse, rather than a polite and firm statement. (We will explore a working statement at the end of this article.)

Oddly enough, people feel free to ask you to justify your fees when these same folks would never dream of asking that rude question of a banker, auto dealer, insurance salesperson, department store clerk or grocery checker! My personal reason for assuming that this question is asked of pet-sitting professionals is that prospects or customers seem to feel that this is a small, home-based business, similar, in their minds, to setting up a booth at a flea market where the buyer is usually free to haggle over the price proffered.

Regardless of your present price structure, you have set fees for your service which are based upon firm principles. You know what kennels charge for boarding. You know what a pet day care charges (if that service exists in your area). You know what your competitors charge for their services. Your fees are based upon profitably operating, maintaining and growing a professional service for your community.

It is not in your best interest to attempt to explain to the inquiring person all the factors that make up your pricing format. It is only important to answer the question in a polite manner which satisfactorily fulfills the curiosity of the questioner.

Standard Pricing

Most professional pet sitting firms publish a standard price list. At the least, most firms have what could be referred to as "standard" pricing for dogs, cats, birds, fish, etc., along with multiples of that same table for households with more than one pet. Some firms have to establish pricing which includes a mileage factor for commuting over long distances. Some firms charge by time spent, rather than number of pets. In almost all cases the same fees apply for similar sittings. That is, if customer "A" lives on one street and has two cats she would be charged the exact same fee as customer "B" who also has two cats and lives within a half-mile of "A".

Many firms who fail during the first year of pet sitting do so because of poor pricing. Prices are either set too low or are determined on each job, at each interview. This means that many or all customers are paying different prices for similar sittings. This can easily lead to a customer's mistrust of the pet sitting firm.

Holding Firm On Pricing

Although it is tempting, at times, to vacillate on pricing, holding firm is the best option. I have passed up many jobs rather than discount my fee schedule. Here are just three reasons you will be happy you remained firm on your pricing:

- You have the assurance that all your customers are paying the same price.
- You are not taking a job at less that your normal, profitable rate.
- You are not open to a "challenge" of your fees because of the discounted pricing.

What Do I Say?

If you have a customer or prospect who asks that bold question, "How did you arrive at the prices you charge for pet sitting?", you can respond with an answer which includes and prevents future questions on the same topic. Here then, is a suggested answer:

"Our pricing is extremely competitive. We keep our prices as low as possible for customers based upon current needs for maintaining our professional service. We have not raised our prices in the past____ (months/years). We will only raise our prices again when the rise in the cost of living and/or inflation make it mandatory. We pride ourselves on giving the best possible service with a minimum amount of staff. (Or…"with just me" if you are the only pet sitter!) We know that your are/will be pleased with our service once you try us."

This answers the question and precludes the inquirer from asking about future price increases when they become necessary.

Whether you choose to use this statement as your response or not, I urge you to make up a statement of your own which you can readily pluck from your memory bank so that you can fully answer the question when it arises. Practice answering the question in front of a mirror, or to a willing family member, until you have it memorized.

Forearmed is forewarned.

Being Our Professional Best

by Lynda J. Foro, Stay 'N Home Pet Sitting

August 1994, Vol.1 Issue 2

"Professional Pet Sitter" describes a growing number of persons being paid for providing in-home animal care. A professional is "engaged in a specific activity as a means of livelihood," says *Webster's II Dictionary.*

If earning money were the only criterion for professionalism, all pet sitters would be equally qualified. What the dictionary adds to the definition of professional is that one possesses "great skill or experience in a field or activity...with assured competence in a field."

Now we're entering the field of qualifiers which becomes more nebulous, "having indefinite form or limits." Without industry standards for performance, pet sitters may be self-proclaimed professionals while having little experience or knowledge to merit the title.

In my pet-sitting brochure, there is a paragraph that addresses several points: my formal education, personal pet ownership, years of pet-sitting experience, and my continuing education in the area of animal issues and animal care.

When we put ourselves in the shoes of a client, we can recognize their comfort at having information about the person who is staying in their home. References obtained will deal only with experiences gained by other clients. Uneventful service may be accidental; a fully qualified pet sitter can handle emergencies whether tested or not.

A pet sitter who demonstrates a willingness to be informed, to be knowledgeable about animal health, to serve as a resource to community services, and who can speak on animal issues comes close to representing the consummate pet-sitting professional.

Whether one functions as a pet-sitting agency or a one-sitter operation, the same demonstration of professionalism is vital to the image of in-home animal care providers.

The need for continuing education cannot be overemphasized. To be competitive in the field and to best serve our clients, we are well advised to read the literature, attend conferences, become acquainted with local shelters and rescue groups, and stay current with animal-related issues.

In this way, we will come closer to the ideal of a professional pet sitter and set an example for others to follow.

In-home animal care is growing as a personal service profession. In time, industry standards will be in place. Certification programs are in the future. For now, we'll have more fun, earn credibility and be knowledgeable about our business if we set our own standards for excellence. When we take pride in our service, we are on the road to being our professional best.

Use Public Speaking As A Business Builder.

by Bill Foster, Paw Partners, Inc.

May 1994, Vol. 1, Issue 1

"What do you do for a living, John?" I asked the burly, 6'2" muscular man.

"Well, Bill, I'm a steel worker. I put up the scaffolding on high-rise buildings. My current project is on the framework of the 54th floor."

"My goodness," I gasped, "I could never do that in a million years. I would be terrified of falling."

John then asked me what I did for a living. "I give sales seminars to groups of twenty or more salespeople," I told him matter-of-factly. John blanched.

"I'll tell you honestly, Bill, I'd rather take a ten-story dive from one of my riggings than speak in front of a group of people."

All of us are afraid of something. Speaking in public is the number one fear in the United States today. Most people will go to any length to avoid facing a room full of strangers and speaking in front of them.

If you have a fear of public speaking, the good news is that you don't have to do it in your business to be successful. The bad news is that public speaking is probably the best free publicity you can ever get for your business.

Within the same month, I gave a four-week seminar for Junior Achievement on business basics, lectured a group of senior citizens on the joys of pet sitting and gave a talk at a local college on humor in pet sitting. Each and every meeting was fun, diverse, unusual and unexpectedly spontaneous. The meetings left me exhausted and exuberant.

I like speaking in front of people, but I didn't start out that way. Enjoying speaking in public is a learned skill. Few people are put on the planet with those natural abilities.

The answer to public speaking is all summed up in three words. Practice. Practice. Practice. You didn't learn to ride a bike or drive a car by only reading a book. You learned both those skills by doing it.

Staying Motivated

by Bud Most, The Iams Company

Jan/Feb 1999, Vol. IV, Issue 1

Being an entrepreneur is the only way to work, right? After all, no one is constantly looking over your shoulder, you can set your own hours, and you can even determine your own salary! Who could want more? Most business owners quickly realize that it's just not that simple. There is always someone looking over your shoulder whether it's your banker, the government, or our competitors. Setting your own working hours usually means being accessible twenty-four hours a day, seven days a week. And determining your salary usually involves scraping up any leftover funds after all the bills are paid.

So, with all the challenges facing an entrepreneur, how do you stay motivated? How do you keep a positive attitude and continually strive to improve? How do you maintain a high level of productivity when your mind keeps telling you, "Enough already?". Read on for a few simple suggestions that have helped me maintain a positive attitude, avoid burnout, and improve job performance.

Know What Drives You

The word "motivation" actually comes from two words: "motive" and "action". Each of us has different personalities and, therefore, different motivators. Look at the following list of motivators and identify the things that inspire you. On a scale of one to ten, give a ten to those things that inspire you the most and a one to the things that almost never get you motivated. Then, identify the five top drivers that give you a motive to take action:

__Time to oneself

__Guarantees

__Family

__Travel/vacation time

__Close, personal friendships

__Wide circle of acquaintances

__Pleasing/serving others

__Power/influence

__Health & fitness

__Successful career

__Fancy/expensive house, car, etc.

__Career advancement

__Earning a lot of money

__Recognition of achievements

__Involvement in key decisions

__Ethical work & lifestyle

__Meaningful work

__Contributing to society

__Excelling in tasks and responsibilities

__Overcoming challenges

__Learning/personal development

__Status

__Other _____

__Other _____

Now that you have a fairly good understanding of your motivators, think of ways you can constantly remind yourself of your motivations.

Picture It

A very good friend and business acquaintance of mine once explained to me his way of staying motivated. George liked his job, even though his supervisor often disagreed with his business strategies. He was a highly productive employee, but he was often perceived as being an individual who would try to find the easiest way to handle a situation. His knowledge and experience often exceeded those of his peers, but he rarely got the credit he deserved. I often wondered how George was able to maintain an optimistic attitude in an environment of pessimism. One day, while we were driving in the rural roads of Florida, George told me his secret. I couldn't believe how simple it was.

George was always a family man. It was clear that his motivators always related to the health and welfare of his family. One of the things he cherished the most was spending the weekends at the lake with his wife and children. He loved taking his family water-skiing but was slightly discouraged by the performance of his boat. The engine had just enough horsepower to pull one skier out of the water and take them down the lake at a very slow speed. He always dreamed of having a new, high-performance boat that would enhance the pleasure he and his family experienced during those special weekends at the lake.

A new boat motivated George to take action and work hard even in an adverse climate. He stayed motivated by simply clipping pictures of the boat of his dreams and placing them in key locations. George had a picture of the boat on his dashboard. He hung one on the mirror in his bathroom so it greeted him every morning. There was even a photo in his appointment book. Every time George would look at his dream boat, he would fantasize of weekends at the lake cruising with his family in a brand new ski boat.

Get pictures of your motivators and place them in strategic locations where you will often see them throughout the day. Picture the outcome of all your efforts, and you will be able to handle even the least motivating of tasks.

Write It Down
Setting goals and identifying accomplishments is one of the best ways I am able to stay motivated. After graduation, I realized that experience was more important to employers than high grades. Therefore, I accepted jobs that allowed me to focus on skills where I gained the most experience –animal care and training.

It was soon obvious to me that my opportunities for promotion were quite limited in the world of dog training. The way to become more successful was to open my own dog training facility or gain exposure using various forms of media. I had no idea how to accomplish either task, so I accepted a truck-driving job that paid better than dog training. Soon, I found myself working to earn a paycheck with no clear direction for the future. I liked the job, but I was constantly depressed and tired.

Fortunately, a company that had a resourceful owner employed me. I soon learned many of the strategies that made him successful. Of all the things he taught me, nothing compares with learning to write down a strategic plan. As I've evolved in the business world, it's clear to me that the most successful and motivated people use this strategy every day of their lives.

A strategic plan is nothing more than identifying where you are today, where you want to go, and how you're going to get there. Many professionals plan, but the successful ones write it down on paper.

Long-Term Planning
This type of plan includes all your top motivators and creates goals (where you want to go). Then, you assess your current conditions (where you are today). Finally, action steps (how you're going to get there) are written to provide a road map to help you achieve those goals.

Your goals must be measurable. That means attaching a date or some other measurement to one of your motivators. For example, one of my motivators is to achieve financial success to support my family after I retire. My goal would read something like, "Obtain $_____ in savings before I reach sixty-seven to maintain my family's quality of life after I retire."

Next, I would evaluate my current financial conditions to see what needs to be done to achieve my goal. This step requires you to be highly objective. Sometimes reality is not pretty. Be honest with yourself and remember that you do not have to share this information with anyone else. The important part is to write it down. I prefer to put this information in the form of a one-page essay.

Finally, list actions that need to occur to achieve your goal. Each action should have an estimated completion date. An example of an action step would be: "Put $10 in a savings account each week." Or, "Investigate investment opportunities by June 30, 2000." List as many steps as you need and work toward completing the tasks before the completion date you identify.

At the end of every day, set five minutes of time aside to reflect on your plan. Evaluate your accomplishments and change any action steps, if necessary. Plan the next day and incorporate any action steps on tomorrow's "to do" list.

I have often benefited from long term planning in both my personal and professional life. It satisfies me to see that I am accomplishing tasks. I'm energized because I have a clear goal and road map to achieve it. It allows me to prioritize the things I value most. Long term planning allows me to have some control over my life.

Short-Term Planning

This type of planning is simply creating a prioritized "to do" list each and every day. I am to the point where I cannot function at one-hundred percent unless I have my task list nearby.

Every evening, I write a list of tasks I need to complete the following day. This includes things I didn't get done today, as well as pre-planned tasks or action steps from my long-term plan. After I create a list of a reasonable amount of tasks, I then prioritize them while thinking of my motivators. When I wake up, I am enthused about being organized and ready to take on the day.

For some reason, I get motivated when I am able to scratch off one of the tasks from the list. And when I review all the scratched off tasks at the end of the day, I feel a sense of satisfaction and accomplishment knowing that I had a very productive day!

Staying motivated is more than taking action and getting things done. It's an attitude and the way we approach life. We can choose to let our environment run our life, or we can choose to take control of it. After all, isn't that one of the reasons you became an entrepreneur? Make a conscious effort to use these tips to avoid burnout and stay motivated. Why not start right now?

Which Came First...?!

By Bill Foster

March/April 1999, Vol. IV, Issue 2

Sometimes I wonder just where unusual behavior with pet owners begins. If you have been pet sitting for any length of time, you have certainly observed unusual feeding instructions and unusual visiting instructions for pets. For example, there was one young lady who told me emphatically that her cat would not eat any food unless I measured out a tablespoon of cooking oil and mixed it thoroughly with the food. Did the cat ask for the cooking oil? What prompted that lady to add the cooking oil to the food in the first place?

Here are a few more examples of weird and unusual requests that I have either received personally or heard about from sitters.

- A lady who insisted that her Bulldog get one-fourth of a jar of dry-roasted peanuts every evening prior to bedtime, or he couldn't sleep. (I didn't take that sitting assignment!)
- A box turtle who would not defecate unless you watched him and stroked his back!
- A Golden Retriever who would only eat one nugget of food at a time, and only if it was hand-fed to him, one nugget at a time!
- A parrot who had to have at least one colored peanut in his mixture of food or he refused to eat. (Oh yes, the color of the peanut had to be green!)
- A Cocker Spaniel who would only eat if his favorite teddy bear was next to the food bowl. (The dog had other teddy bears but this was a special one.)
- A cat whose owner placed six different kinds of food on the floor each night so the cat could decide what she liked to eat and had variety each night.
- A Dachshund who cannot sleep at night unless he is wrapped up in his blanket with only his nose and eyes sticking out...looking like the wolf in Little Red Riding Hood.

The last example, the Dachshund, belongs to me! Yes, I am guilty of furnishing our Dachshund, Pancho, with his favorite blanket and he roots around until he is completely wrapped in the blanket with only his face partially sticking out. I noticed his obsession with the blanket when he was only a baby and it continues to this day. My fault entirely.

During your sitting experience you have probably noticed that these odd requests or special instructions from owners usually come as an afterthought to the main instructions. I believe this is because the unusual behavior is more important to the humans than to the pets. We believe our pets to be members of our family, and we want to allow them to have some of the same quirks and foibles that we have in our own lives.

If you can top my "odd requests" from customers, PSI would love to hear from you. We'll print as many as possible in upcoming issues of *The WORLD*.

Y2K and Pet Sitting

by Lani Stites

May/June 1999, Vol. IV, Issue 3

I'm tired of hearing about Y2K and the Millennium Bug. The doomsayers are predicting everything from panic to riots to anarchy. My computer is a Macintosh, so I'm not worried. Since I live in earthquake country, we have disaster supplies already in place for our family and pets, so I'm not worried.

But, will Y2K affect my pet sitting business? Will business be slow during the last week of the century because owners don't want to be away, or owners have to work like so many banks, etc. are doing? Will my clients have enough pet food, water and other things to make it possible to do my job if they are stranded out of town longer than expected? And, what about the "crazies" who will be out there on the highways and by-ways during the last week of the year? Those same highways that all pet sitters have to drive on a daily basis? Resignedly, I decided to do some research, and I have put in some serious hours of deliberation on the subject. I also attended a local Y2K meeting. As a result, I have decided to use an old cliché - "Expect the best, but prepare for the worst".

I am happy to share the following time line that I am putting into effect for my pet sitting business and Y2K. Please Note: This article does not cover basic disaster preparedness for you or your family. That is a separate issue. I also am not addressing whether or not you should restrict reservations during this time or charge extra for sits on this holiday. That is something sitters need to decide for themselves.

Early Summer

- Experts are suggesting we have cash on hand at the end of the year. The amount is anywhere from $40 to $4,000. It is a good idea to get the money you want to have at this time of year to avoid long lines and cash shortages that are expected at the end of December. One suggestion is to get travelers checks or put the cash in a safety deposit box. One bank official told me they were totally equipped to handle anything that the bug would bring. But just in case, they are printing out all account information before the end of the year so that bank transactions could be done by hand if computers do fail.

- Send out a newsletter or fliers to your clients about Y2K. This could include (1) shopping lists for owners to buy supplies for their pets now and store them for later, (2) security information on making their homes safe from thieves, and (3) securing a paper copy of their pet's vet records now. In case the veterinarian's computer does crash, the pet sitter will have proof of vaccinations for animal control or emergency treatment. Sources of shopping lists and other disaster preparedness tips: Red Cross, EARS (Emergency Animal Rescue Service) and FEMA (Federal Emergency Management Agency.

Early Fall

- After the summer rush is over, give some consideration to a Y2K clause in your contracts for the end of December and beginning of January. Things to include in a Y2K clause:

  a. Alternative communications. If the telephone lines are out, maybe give clients a cell phone number.

  b. Request that owners have a sufficient supply of food, water and medicines for all pets in case they are not able to return on the expected date.

  c. Add something similar to this: "Every effort will be made by the sitter to make the scheduled sits. In the case of infrastructure failure or restricted movement, sitters will attemp other alternatives such as contacting family or neighbors to check on the pets."

  d. Ask the client for a contingency plan or alternative boarding or kenneling if the sitter is unable to make it.

  e. If you are still not sure about your computer, test it now. Many Web sites offer a free device for downloading that will check for the Millennium Bug.

- Now would be a good time to print out any business materials you may need at the beginning of the year; i.e., stationary, contracts, statements and envelopes.

- Is your business phone electric? I have an answering machine and phone combined, and when the electricity goes out, the phone will not ring. So, I bought a cheap phone and when the electricity goes off, the phone lines still work, I can at least have one business line available. Buy a non-electric phone now.

As soon as you start taking reservations for the end of the year:

- Remind regular clients of shopping lists and records needed.
- Get the Y2K clause signed.

When picking up keys from new clients for the end of the year:

- Give newsletter or shopping lists to new clients.
- Have Y2K clause signed.

Week of December 26-31

- In my opinion, this will be the worst of the whole scenario. Instead of long lines at the mall to return gifts, the long lines will be at the grocery stores, banks and gas stations.
- Consider storing extra gas in safe, five-gallon gas cans.
- Avoid city centers or other areas where traffic may be congested. Build in extra-drive time cushions.
- Above all, stay calm. Plan extra coffee breaks or alone time to deal with the stress and panic that others may be creating around you. Let's be careful out there!

I heard the story of one family who has purchased property up in the mountains and will be heading there the day after Christmas. They have extra food and supplies, and then have even gone so far as buying a horse and wagon for transportation. Let's hope the worst/best that will happen is that they will need a pet sitter to feed the horse because no disaster strikes at midnight on December 31st and they are able to return home.

Disaster Planning

Recent events have brought disaster planning to the forefront of the news. From terrorist attacks to natural disasters, the need to plan for disaster before it happens has been a hot topic of the 21st Century.

But well before this, *The WORLD* was advising pet sitters on the importance of preparation for earthquakes, hurricanes and other disastrous situations. The information and advice in its pages has ensured the safekeeping—and doubtless saved the lives—of many, many beloved pets.

Expect the Unexpected:
Disaster Planning for the Pet Sitter

by Diana Guerrero

Fall 1996, Vol. III, Issue 4

For some reason, I woke up. I turned around to look at the clock and it was 4:48 a.m. A couple seconds later, both dogs I was pet-sitting ran into the room. I got up as they braced themselves. I lunged to grab the door, and as I did, the whole house began to lurch and rock. Since the house was partially on stilts, located over the side of the mountain, I feared we might slide down into the gully below.

After what seemed like an eternity, the house stopped moving. My first thought was about my own pets. Nobody was with my dog at my house, which was across the mountainous pass. I turned on the news and attempted to call my assistant and some other people before the phone lines were swamped. I managed to leave a couple messages and prepared to leave.

On this early morning of June 28, 1992, I was thankful that I had included a disaster plan in my original business plan and always insisted on keeping current with it. So, clients' emergency contacts were always on alert when my clients were gone, and I was visiting their homes and pets.

As I tried to leave, my truck would not start. I disengaged the battery. Shortly after, another quake hit. This one was close. Had I been on the road, I would have been crushed in the rockslide on a road called the Arctic Circle. I later discovered that three access roads to my home were closed.

Fortunately, at the time of the quake, I had food and water in my vehicle and had a full tank of gas. Shortly after the quake, gas was sold out and the stores were mobbed with people gathering food and water.

Monitoring the media reports, which were horrible, only made me crazy. Finally, one of the roads was opened for residents. I drove almost four hours to get back to my community (normally a 40 minute trip)...to start searching the rubble for my client's pets. I had to trust that my assistant had gotten my dog out safely.

Any disaster shakes you up - this one did so, literally. It was fortunate that I had one of the lightest schedules in a long time with only a handful of clients out of town. All but one were indoor felines. All their emergency contacts had already been in to check the security and turn off utilities. My job was to assess the conditions of the animals and the property.

The first house I entered was a nightmare. The stove was tipped up and balancing only because the plug was holding it up. It had moved forward about four feet. Glass covered the floors and counters of the kitchen. Cabinets and drawers were a mess. The cat had disappeared.

I began a systematic search, starting with one room and working through it before closing if off and going to another. She was not in any of her normal hiding places, and she would not answer me.

Finally, I checked in the little open area near the motor of the refrigerator. There she was, her eyes were fully dilated and she was not going to move. Since the house was intact and she was fine, I moved her food and litterbox into the area adjacent to the fridge. She was fine for now and would be okay. I left her for the next house.

The next house was in pretty good shape. Some of the artwork was dislodged from the wall and there was a mess, as the refrigerator contents spilled all over the floor. There was a note from the emergency contact, who had already been in to check, saying all was okay. I did a quick overview and found an electric razor in the toilet tank, along with spilled drugs and things. The electricity had been shut off and I closed the door to prevent animal access to that area. The cat was hiding behind the washer and came when I called. During the aftershock periods, he hid under the bedspread in the room of his owners. I visited with him for a bit and went out to check on the dogs. All the dogs were fine—not fazed at all. The fence was intact and since all was secure, I moved on, as the daylight hours were fast coming to an end.

In the next several houses, I found varying degrees of damage, but I began to feel better. Things could have been worse. So far, all the houses were standing (no broken windows or collapsed gates, doors or fences for animals to escape out of) and the animals were fine.

When I arrived at the last house, my heart sank. The home was owned by one of the few millionaire clients I had. It was dusk and there was an eerie light cast on the home, and I knew I had to work fast. The house was two stories and extensive. When I got into the house, I couldn't believe it. It was located less that a mile from the earthquake's epicenter. Of all the homes I had been in, this was the worst.

The two cats that lived there were complete opposites. One was my bosom buddy and came right to me when he heard the door open. I had to pick him up since he walking all over broken glass and I was afraid he would cut himself.

The chimney was cracked and the grandfather clock had fallen face down across the entryway. Televisions lay on the floor and the kitchen looked like a bomb had gone off. Fluorescent lights and covers lay on the floor, along with the china, glassware, contents of the refrigerator, and other assorted goodies from the cupboard. Water was dripping from the dispenser in the fridge and the ceiling was dripping water.

I crated the cat, went to check on the water source and began my search for the remaining cat.

The water source was a hot water tank that had fallen over upstairs. It had destroyed the antique table below and damaged the flooring. The water was off and there wasn't much more I could do.

I began my search. First, I began by checking all the normal hiding places. As I looked in a closet, my heart stopped. The cream color fur was only just exposed. As I diligently searched in the closet, now only dimly lit with my flashlight, I uncovered the (empty) FURRY SKI BOOT! Thank God! (The cat was later found, safe and sound!)

After surviving this upsetting experience, a fellow Rotarian asked me to contribute to the community disaster plan because of my knowledge as an animal behavior expert and my planning and experiences. I got whisked away into the animal disaster planning community. The role has made me well known in the area. And, in addition to writing a community plan, I have done pro-active workshops and seminars on the topic for pet sitters and other pet professionals, including zoological facilities.

To the pet sitting professional, I cannot stress enough the importance of emergency or disaster planning. I would also recommend thinking long and hard about what you **will** and **will not** do in case of an emergency.

Here are a few tips:

- Have personal, business, neighborhood and community plans for emergencies and disasters.
- Expect no help from your staff. They may be homeless or dealing with their own problems. What will be reasonable? How far will you stretch your business neck out?
- Have emergency kits in your vehicles. Instruct clients in kit and carrier needs.
- Have an emergency plan that covers your clients and you. Consider all times of the day or night and whether you are on the road, home or elsewhere.
- Always carry a crow bar, first aid kit, wrench, manual can opener, flashlight (with working batteries), gloves, extra leashes and lead ropes in your car. Also, a car emergency kit is recommended. Highly advisable is a tape recorder with tape and batteries. This can be used to record important phone numbers and information for later if you are driving, especially in emergencies when people are disoriented and panicked.
- Never put your keys down. Keep them on your body or hooked to you.
- Practice systematic planning for procedures or searches.
- How will clients contact you in an emergency? What if phones are down?
- Do not overbook.
- Be realistic, not complacent.

When Pet-Sitting Becomes Pet Saving

by Bonnie Brayshaw, Assistant Coordinator of Communications, United Animal Nations' Emergency Animal Rescue Services

Fall 1996, Vol. III, Issue 4

Well, it's the big holiday weekend and, thanks to your hard-won, well-deserved reputation, you're booked solid—caring for the Garrett's Shetland ponies, Father Donaldson's reticulated python, your college chum Fast Eddie's macaws and Mrs. Biddle's terrier terrorists, among others. Friday evening, after lavishing equal amounts of loving care on the Simmons' Somali grand champion and the Williams' ancient diabetic mutt, you crank up the oldies station in your car, singing all the way home, convinced you've got the best job in the world.

At 2:30 a.m. Saturday, the unthinkable happens-earthquake! In the pitch-black night filled with screams and sirens, you comfort your own animals as your thoughts race frantically from the little Biddles (who've certainly demolished their house if the quake didn't do it) to the ponies (will you be able to make it out to the stables?) to poor old Muggsy (who's *got* to have insulin in a few hours). What are you going to do?

You need a disaster plan *now*, and to implement an effective one, you'll need to do some brain work and leg work right away.

What's the Worst that Can Happen?

There's no way to plan for all the threats and hardships of a disaster, but a good plan can take you far if it's thorough, yet flexible enough to adapt to whatever happens. Start yours by pinpointing the types of catastrophes your community is most likely to experience. Review this list:

Natural Disasters

Avalanche	Blizzard
Mud slide	Sink hole
Drought	Earthquake
Flood	Hurricane
Lightning strike	Storm surge
Tidal wave	Tornado
Volcano eruption	Wildfire

Man-made Disasters

Airplane crash	Building collapse
Car or truck accident	Chemical spill
Explosion	Oil spill
House fire	Riots
Boat sinking	Train derailment
Broken gas main	War

They can't *all* happen where you live; many won't affect all of your community and clients; and many of the plans you're going to make will apply no matter what calamities hit your hometown.

Big Questions

Now, for each potential disaster, do your best to come up with answers to these vital question.

- How will I travel to my clients' animals?
- How will I feed the animals with all the stores closed?
- How will I provide safe shelter and care for my clients' animals?
- How will I let my clients know what's become of their animals?
- How will I get medical treatment for injured animals?

Starting to look impossible? Probably is - working alone. But you're going to enlist the help of many good people.

- Yourself, your family and friends
- Your clients
- Your community's animal people (vets, shelters, fellow pet sitters, pet care stores, boarding kennels, etc.)

Put a Plan on Paper

Before you discuss your plan with others, though, begin preparing yourself. Get a big notebook and label it "Disaster Plan." Organize it in logical sections - what you're going to do, supplies you have and their locations, etc. Create a section that names the people who've agreed to help you. Include their phone numbers (home, work, car and beepers), addresses, directions to their houses, how they're going to help, etc. Add a section for the emergency phone numbers and the radio stations that broadcast disaster updates. Be sure you write everything down somewhere because you may not be thinking clearly during the disaster —don't depend on your memory! Don't depend on having electrical power either. If you write up your plan on your computer, be sure you always keep at least two current hardcopies- one in your home or office and one stored with your disaster survival kit.

Pack a Disaster Survival Kit

In an airline crate, an old suitcase or a plastic storage box, stash as many of these supplies as you can:

• Your disaster plan	• Pocket knife
• Animal first aid books	• Backpack
• Extra leashes and collars	• Blankets
• Emergency phone numbers	• Food & water dishes
• Heavy gloves	• Paper & cloth towels
• Manual Can opener	• Animal first aid kit
• Map and street guides	• Plastic bags - all sizes
• Animal medicines	• Muzzles
• Spoons for food	• Bleach or disinfectant
• Kitty litter	• Bottled water
• Copies of client records	• Flashlight & batteries
• Plastic or rubber gloves	• Plastic tarp
• Dog stakes and cables	• Fire extinguisher
• Evac sack (for cats)	• Small litter boxes
• Extra food	• Flea spray

Make up some lost-animal posters, leaving blanks for information you won't have right now. If an animal in your care is lost, you'll have posters ready to fill in and distribute throughout the area where the animal escaped.

Keep your kit handy in the garage or car trunk, replacing outdated supplies and batteries promptly.

Inventory your personal "property", considering how it might be used in a disaster. Besides animal care supplies and equipment, perhaps you have:

- Hi-tech communicators—cellular phones, car phones, CB radios, beeper
- Camping gear—tents, portable stoves, lanterns, sleeping bags, tarps
- Vehicles—4-wheel drive trucks or vans, campers, boats, bicycle, motorcycles - even a snowmobile might come in handy!
- Sporting equipment—sturdy shoes, biking helmets, knee and elbow pads, boating or scuba equipment

Of course you don't own all this, that's why, as Bette Midler says,"Ya Got to Have Friends." You certainly know folks who have some of this stuff. Ask if they'll loan it. And what about clients or friends who own kennels or pasture land? Would they let you house animals on their property in an emergency? That retired cabinet maker you pet sit for - would he be willing to knock together some emergency shelters if needed? Could your daughter's scout troop carry food by bicycles to animals if roads were impassable? Talk to these folks now. Be certain they understand what you're asking and how you'll contact them. Then, go home and write all the information up in your disaster plan.

Prepare your Clients

Next, get to work on your clients. Along with the usual travel itineraries and emergency phone numbers, start asking them to leave the following items for you in a waterproof zip-close plastic bag:

- Recent photos of each animal
- A copy of each animal's medical record
- Written permission to get emergency medical attention for their pet in their absence
- Notes on the animal's typical reactions to stress and favorite hiding place
- Names of friends/family who live out of the immediate area and who would be willing to temporarily house their animal if it's displaced by a disaster.
- A means to transport each animal - cage or crate for house pets; trailer, hitch, and possibly something to pull it with for horses, llamas, ostriches, etc.

Tour clients' homes with an eye for disaster safety. Suggest they move aquariums and caged animals away from things that might fall on them. Encourage them to secure cages to walls with hooks and eyes, making sure the doors fasten securely. During Hurricane Andrew, many birdcages fell or were smashed and many opportunistic kitties dined on valuable and beloved parrots.

Suggest that clients move dog houses and runs from beneath heavy tree branches, chimneys, brick or cinderblock fences, etc. - making sure there's still plenty of shade in the new location. Ask that each animal wear a collar and tag with up-to-date information, including both address and phone number. Suggest microchipping as a more permanent form of identification.

Encourage clients to attend neighborhood crime-watch team meetings. These folks are already looking out for each other; during a disaster, they'd most certainly be willing to check on or feed animal neighbors until you can get there. Suggest they compile and distribute a list of the number and type of animals at each home in their neighborhood.

Give clients a written summary of your disaster plan and your recommendations for keeping pets safe. Explain that, if necessary to evacuate their animals, you'll post signs in their house telling where you've taken them. Be sure they know you've already networked with others in your community to ensure the best possible care for their pets.

Prepare Your Community

Talk to your local animal shelters - do they have a disaster plan? If so, how is the community figured into it? Find out what resources they have that you could use during a disaster. Will they board displaced animals? For how long? Will they charge for it? Will they provide free pet food and water to the public? Have they arranged for a vet on-site to treat injured pets? Ask many of these same questions of local vets. Are they prepared to help in a disaster? Are they aware of, or members of, the AMA's Emergency Response Force?

Then there's kennels and pet care stores. Will they cooperate with you? Loan you supplies? Extend credit? Provide you with animal housing or services?

One of the best ways to prepare yourself for disaster is training. United Animal Nation's Emergency Animal Rescue Service conducts day-long volunteer training workshops all over the country teaching people to respond to the needs of animals during disasters. Sign up! For more information, contact UAN at 916-429-2457. Consider Red Cross Disaster and first aid training as well.

Stay Ready!

Once your plan is in place, review and revise it from time to time. Have other emergency responders look it over, and stay prepared mentally. When the dam breaks or a tornado rips through town, keep cool, resourceful and refer often to your plan.

Acknowledge that, in a major disaster, you probably won't save every animal. No one could. Do the best you can, not neglecting your own animals or yourself, either. With preparation and determination, you'll make a difference.

Networking

Networking within the pet-sitting industry can be one of the most helpful business-building tools a pet sitter has. It is a source of support, education, information, community outreach and even backup in the event of an illness, injury or family emergency in a pet sitter's life.

It's an unfortunate fact that many pet sitters deprive themselves of this wonderful means of support because they view all other sitters as "competition." *The WORLD has worked very hard from its inception to dispel that notion and to show PSI members the long list of benefits to be found in networking.*

The Benefits of Networking

by Judi Smith, Angelic Pet Sitters, Inc.

Jan/Feb 1997 Vol IV, Issue 1

When I started my pet sitting business, the only full-time professional pet sitter I knew was Nancy Petrone, the owner of PGA Pet Pals, Inc.

 Nancy and I met at a dog training class. When she learned that I had started a pet sitting business, she asked me to assist her when she needed extra help. She also sent me referrals that were out of her area, and in turn, I referred potential clients in her area.

During the first year I operated my business, I serviced clients within a wide range. In October of 1995, we had heavy rains and flooding in much of Palm Beach County. After spending three hours going to and returning from the Wellington (normally a 25 minute drive) due to the flooding, I knew I had to concentrate my efforts in a smaller geographical area. I called Tom Benken, the owner of *A Trusted Friend,* to ask if he would be interested in servicing my Wellington clients. Tom told me that he had a client in my neighborhood he was servicing now and had experienced the same travel problems because of the flooding. We decided to meet for coffee. I invited Nancy Petrone to join us. I had seen Pat Venezio's (Pat's Pet Care) brochures and knew she was a member of PSI and serviced the Jupiter/Tequesta area. I called Pat and invited her to join us.

The first meeting was a success. We all share the same professional standards. Pet sitting is our full-time business. We service different areas of Palm Beach County. We all are members of a professional pet sitting organization. We decided to refer potential clients to the pet sitting service closest to their location rather than each of us attempting to service a large area.

Our clients also benefit from networking among pet sitters. We can provide back up service for vacations and emergencies with another pet sitting service. If a client moves to another area of Palm Beach County, we can refer her to a pet sitter we personally know. I have referred clients moving out of the area to pet sitting services listed in the PSI national directory, and I have received referrals in return from other PSI members.

We recently shared a booth at "Paws for a Cause," a pet related event sponsored by the American Lung Association to promote clean air for pets and people. In addition to sharing booth space, we distributed information about the event to vets and groomers in our individual market areas. The event was a huge success. We benefited by sharing the cost and work to put a booth together. Alone, none of us would have had the time or the money to put together a professional display. The American Lung Association also benefited from our joint efforts in distributing information about the event to our clients, vets and other pet professionals.

A year after our first meeting, we are still working together and have all had occasion to exchange referrals and information with other pet sitting services in addition to our original group. We also network with other pet-related businesses. Networking helps our individual business grow, while matching the client with the services that can best meet his or her needs.

Is There a Catch?

by Cathy Jones, PSI

March/April 1997 Vol II Issue 2

Some pet sitters hesitate to join a network because they fear hidden motives in the networking idea…they fear a catch! If they joined a network, would their promotional ideas be used by other pet sitters? Would other pet sitters utilize their secrets for saving time, building clientele, increasing profits or caring for pets? **WE HOPE SO!**

The point of networking is exactly that – uniting people with similar objectives to find ways of sharing ideas that create business and reduce burn-out. Networking is a two-way process that works. Individually, and as a group, you exchange skills and expertise with your networking partners. You build better service for your clients by referring calls to pet sitters in other areas or even to "competitor" pet sitters when you just can't make another visit. Your partners do the same for you. You also blend your costs by sharing advice on advertising, insurance, community pet-care services and other information that makes you a better service provider and business person. Mostly, you come together with others who understand what you do and why you do it.

PSI would like to encourage you to get involved in your local network. Just like the theme for *Quest for Excellence 1997*, since you are playing anyway, you might as well …*PLAY TO WIN!*

What's In It For You?

by Janice Leaman

Summer 1996 Vol. III, Issue 3

When I first started my business, Tender Loving Cat Care Inc., in June of 1988, I did what any good business person would do. I checked out the competition. Following James Earl Jones' advice, I figured the best place to start was the Yellow Pages. There were approximately fifteen different listings for pet sitters at the time, and I called up a few to introduce myself.

The response I received from other pet sitters was mixed, at best. I came away feeling that most were a little suspicious of me and wondered what my motives were. I wasn't after their business secrets, and I certainly wasn't after their clients. I just wanted them to know that I was new to the business and perhaps we could have a friendly lunch and get to know each other. After such a lukewarm response, I figured pet sitters were not a very amicable bunch.

My wonderful, cynical, practical husband commented that it was a dog-eat-dog world out there (yeah, he can be pretty cute at times), and that owning your own business wasn't for wimps. I replied that I wasn't a wimp; I was just a nice person who wanted to care for cats and dogs and meet others who do the same. He responded with, "Most people want to know what's in it for them." Feeling discouraged and naïve, I quit calling.

I joined a few associations, such as the Women's Business Organization and our local Home-Based Business Association. They talked quite a bit about "networking", about making connections with and supporting other businesses who were growing and struggling just as I was. At one of the many functions, I happened to sit next to an accountant who was looking for a pet sitter. Instant client! And, if I had been looking for an accountant, I definitely would have considered her. Still, despite the help and motivation these organizations gave me, no one really understood MY business. Even worse, I often encountered, "So you, uh pet sit...hmmm, what a sweet little hobby you have, dear."

After I had been in business for nearly a year, I met a lovely lady, Miriam Coco of Fur, Fins, and Feathers, Inc., who had recently started her own pet sitting business. At last, I had found someone who was not "threatened" by little ole me, and who wanted to have lunch and exchange ideas. (And, as stated above, I had so longed to "do lunch.") We met, talked quite a long time about pets, people, and how we could actually make a living doing this. And I came away from our informal meeting with a sense that she **understood** the joys and difficulties of my chosen career because she had been through the same things. We laughed about our clients from hell, the perils of ankle-biting Chihuahuas, and razor-tipped cats. I gave her the name of my insurance agent (who offered a better policy for less money), and she told me about advertising campaigns she had tried that didn't work.

Over the years, we have saved each other money (yes the "M" word), given each other support, and had some great meals in the process. We have even had "high tea" at the Ritz Carlton and continue to have dinner every December at an expensive French restaurant before Christmas season begins in earnest. We also warn each other about "crazy" clients who may be calling, and which pet sitters **not** to hire. We both service Montgomery County, Maryland, but we are most definitely **friendly** competitors.

We truly wondered, though, whether we were in the minority. Miriam's contacts with other sitting services had been similar to mine. Were other sitters as virtuous as we were, or were they a strange, pooper scooper toting bunch bent on degrading the competition and spreading slanderous tales about each other? Were they regular people who happened to love pets, or did they sleep out in the dog runs and bathe in flea dip?

We bit the bullet and tried again. In nearby Northern Virginia, we found a pet sitter who was not only willing to talk to us, she wanted to (yes, you guessed it) have **lunch**. Cynthia Elkey of Alternative Pet Care had been in business for more than eight years (a real pioneer in the early eighties) and she suggested that we invite several more pet sitters in the area that she knew. And, to my and Miriam's delight, these people were **normal**. And they were willing to share valuable information and experience. We came away from our informal meeting with thankful hearts, not to mention some sound advice.

At our luncheon, I had met pet sitters that were just starting up, as well as seasoned pet sitters who had been in business for ages. Most of the companies were one-person operations, but some had employees or used independent contractors. Some talked about the long hours and the constant battle with fatigue. Others talked about juggling pet sitting with child care or other jobs and spouses who were not supportive. I could learn from them all, and sometimes I could even contribute an idea that no one else had thought of. However, we didn't always talk business. Some sitters told us they had actually been able to go on vacations; a worthy goal I continually strive to attain.

We were, in fact, networking. And speaking of networking, how often do you get a call from someone you cannot service? Maybe the client is out of the area you normally cover. Maybe they have a pet who has particular needs or requirements that you cannot handle. Maybe you are totally booked for the holidays. What do you do? If you or your company cannot handle a customer for whatever reason, it is the professional person's responsibility to try and help that caller out.

At the present time, my company employs about fifty pet sitters, however, there are STILL many times when we cannot meet a potential customer's needs. In the Washington, DC, area (near which we are located), there are probably no less than a hundred pet sitting services. So, when my company isn't able to help a caller, I refer the person to another business whose owner I have either personally met or at least spoken to at length on the phone. And guess what? They refer clients back to me when they are unable to do a job. I have acquired more new customers this way than through many other advertising strategies. All this for the price of a meal!

Having an organization like Pet Sitters International gives us all a clue as to who the serious, committed pet sitters are. And, since I am sure that PSI members are devouring each issue of *The WORLD of Professional Pet Sitting* from cover to cover, not to mention attending yearly conferences, we are without a doubt a much better educated group of people than non-affiliated pet sitters. So, gather up your courage and pick up the phone! Call your fellow PSI members to set up a lunch at a central place or plan a trip to a local attraction. In the Washington, DC, area, we have been to the zoo, traveled to a nearby winery, toured a mansion, and had a picnic.

I know that pet sitters are an exceptionally busy group, but try hard to take a few hours to meet your "fellow pet people." Give your spouse, your sister, or your good friend your dog walks for the day. With a much needed break, you might be easier to live with and the rewards can be tremendous. If there aren't any PSI members in your immediate vicinity, remember telephone conversations with pet sitters in other parts of the country can achieve similar results for the participants.

Lastly, don't forget to tell the other pet sitters in your area who are not members, about PSI. Educating other pet sitters and encouraging them to have high ethics and standards can only help the pet sitting industry. That, in turn, can only help you. We are all entrepreneurs making our way in a demanding world. What's in it for your? A better business!

Member to Member
The Sitter to Sitter Series
Bright Ideas

Member to Member

Been there, done that—The Voice of Experience speaks louder than most other sources of advice and information. This was especially true in an industry as new as pet sitting was in those early years. It also means more in our industry where PSI members are dealing with their clients' beloved "fur children."

There is a special bond among pet sitters that is best described in the following pages where pet sitters speak directly to other pet sitters about the ups and downs, problems and joys of being a professional pet sitter.

Member to Member

Jan/Feb 1997 Vol. IV, Issue 1

Members shared the following tips on how pet sitters can better attend to personal appearance so as to make a good first impression at client interviews:

- I note quickly when entering the home if folks remove their shoes at the door. If it appears so, I offer to do the same. People are impressed that you noticed.

- We always schedule consultation between rounds, so that we may shower and change first. If a last minute need arises, we explain to the new client that we will have to meet them "in uniform."

- A lint brush, sticky roller, change of shoes, fresh shirt with business name and logo, brush, hairspray, lip gloss and mirror kept together allows me to freshen up before going to meet new customers.

- I treated myself to makeover and glamour photo. One of the photos I did in a black blazer, and I keep it on file in case the newspaper wants a photo. I felt so great and it was fun!

- All of our pet sitters wear a work smock in our company color, royal blue, embroidered with our company name and logo. The smock protects clothing from pet hair and dirt and can be easily removed when running errands or going on client interviews.

How Pet Sitters Can Make a Difference

May 1995 Vol. II, Issue 2

In the February '95 *WORLD,* we asked members for ways that professional pet sitters could make a difference in the pet world-especially concerning the spay/neuter effort. As we expected, you had some really good ideas which included the following:

- Make it standard practice to ask if all clients' pets are fixed. If not, pursue the issue with them. Back up your talk with hard facts/statistics from your city or county. Many people are unaware of the problem caused by animals that aren't fixed.

- Have a list of low cost spay/neuter programs that are available in your area to leave with clients.

- I put "Have your pets spayed or neutered" on my answering machine greeting and it is also on my magnetic car signs.

- Write an article in your company's newsletter about pet overpopulation and put statistics in it as to how many cats and dogs have to be put down by vets, shelters, etc. each year because there are more animals than there are homes for.

- Often pet owners find that their pets don't like certain foods that have been bought for them. Pet sitters can offer to take these foods along with old rugs to the local pet shelter where they'll be put to good use.

- Develop a program with your local shelter to run ads in the local paper showing animals to be adopted and include something about your company; i.e. "Adopt one of these precious animals presently located at the _____ animal shelter and receive a free pet-sitting visit from _____."

The Power To Make A Difference: Professional Pet Sitters!

by Lynda Foro

February 1995 Vol. II, Issue 1

Pet Sitters, by definition, care for pets. What sets us apart is that we care about pets, as well. To this end, most of us share a concern for the crisis of dog and cat overpopulation.

Many PSI members take an active role in trying to alleviate the suffering of homeless and unwanted animals. Individuals and organized groups perform rescue operations for feral cats, desperately trying to spay and neuter their colonies. Homeless dogs are equally heartbreaking, but their numbers are less visible due to community-sponsored animal control and aggressive euthanasia policies.

Most humane professionals agree that a universal spay and neuter program is the answer to the problem of increasing numbers of unwanted animals. The social tragedy of homeless, suffering animals and the havoc they can cause in a community goes unchecked without intervention. For this reason, community education and a coordinated effort to sterilize dogs and cats, pets or otherwise, is endorsed by countless animal welfare organizations.

Programs are developing in many communities to facilitate access to low-cost spay and neuter clinics. Local efforts are growing through the cooperation of caring veterinarians and dedicated citizens, humane societies, shelters, animal rescue groups and animal advocates are united in the concept of preventing unwanted animal births.

According to Patti Moran, founder and coordinator, Pet Sitters International recognizes the pet overpopulation crisis that exists in the United States today and strongly endorses the spay/neuter effort. As in-home animal care providers, pet sitters are in a unique position to make a difference. PSI members can educate their clients to the necessity of sterilizing their animals. By whatever method is most comfortable - pet sitters can passively make literature available or aggressively talk with clients about this issue- we have the opportunity to educate and persuade the public.

Whether we work cooperatively though Pet Sitters International or individually in our own communities, professional pet sitters can exercise social responsibility and make a difference in combating the pet overpopulation problem. As Patti says, how wonderful it would be to have every dog or cat be a wanted pet-who has a pet sitter.

First Impressions: The Importance of a Professional Appearance

by Kate Barclay, Kozy Kritters

Fall 1996 Vol III Issue 4

Where does the day go? Walk Martie, Spunky, Stumpy, Bear and Lady. Feed and give hugs to Miss Kitty, Spooky, Orbit 8 and find time for a mental-health coffee break. One during which I didn't have to share a muffin with a furry guy. Checking my calendar for the day, I realize Amy Jenkins is expecting me for a home visit within 30 minutes. Holy Moley, I am a wreck! Well, I work with animals and she surely doesn't expect me to show up in a business suit. I'll just mention that I came over from my daily dog walks. She'll understand. After all, what does she expect?

My home visit took the normal allotted time. She was a really nice person and seemed to understand that I was not as clean and neat as usual. Her two dogs and one kitty were super friendly and, oh boy, these pets are gonna be fun. Great job, easy money. Except...I didn't get that great pet-sitting engagement. It was awarded to another sitter.

Amy was kind enough to share with me her thoughts and concerns. She really liked me as a "person" and felt that I may be capable of giving her pets, who adored me, excellent care.

Amy's concerns lay elsewhere. Amy felt that my "personal appearance" reflected a careless attitude. Wow, was I set back.

I asked how the other sitter's presentation was exceptional over my presentation. It was noted that all things were the same with one exception-the other sitter was neat, clean, and wore (minimal) make-up. This sitter made the pet owner feel confident that she cared for herself as a professional, was mature and would transfer that personal care and self-respect to the care of the client's home and pets.

It is understood that in working with animals we may get covered with muddy pawprints and multicolored fur. It can also make a slovenly statement - I am careless about my personal appearance, therefore I may not be as careful with a pet owner's home and pets' care.

It is not unusual for pet sitters to get distracted with pet care-that is what we do as professional pet care providers. Nor is it unusual for us to forget to set aside a little extra time for ourselves. It is now my practice to take a minute to put an emergency make-up bag in my pet-care backpack to make it easier for me to freshen-up before going into a home visit. On days that I do have a meeting with a pet owner, I include a clean sweater, shirt, t-shirt or something to make me look neat and clean when I meet the pets and pet owners. Professionals care about themselves and present themselves as ambassadors of their industry.

I want to get the job every time I make a home visit. More importantly, I want every pet owner to know that I am a professional, and as such I exemplify the philosophy that pet sitters reflect a professional image for in-home pet care and take great pride in the confidence awarded for the privilege of caring for each pet and its home.

Readers Exchange

by Suzi Hosking, For the Love of Pets

Jan/Feb 1997, Vol. IV, Issue 1

While I am always kept informed and entertained by the pages of *The WORLD,* I was especially interested in Kate Barclay's item (Fall 1996, pg. 15), "First Impressions: The Importance of a Professional Appearance."

I must say that I certainly agree with her 100 percent. I have often been faced with making that horrid decision: The "Go-As-I-Am Look" or the "Stop-Change-and-Freshen-Up Look." Occasionally, there may be little choice. However, I would like to share another viewpoint with our readers and members; one which has been my experience on more than a few occasions when meeting a client for that all-important "initial pre-visit." as I call it.

Kate's comment, "It is understood that in working with animals we may get covered with muddy pawprints and multi-colored fur..." is accurate in itself. However, "It can also make a slovenly statement—I am careless about my personal appearance, therefore, I may not be as careful with a pet owner's home and pets' care," may be the opinion of a select number of fastidious clients.

I have been fortunate that while meeting perspective clients, I have been a great judge of character, simply by speaking with them on the telephone when explaining my service and setting up the pre-visit. Spending a few extra moments on the phone helps me determine their personal situation and attitude concerning their home and their companion animals.

As with many sitting services, my clients range from the casual bachelor whose apartment is always in disarray to the top-notch, white collar executives in a perfectly decorated million-dollar estate. The "outsider" might presume that my attire and appearance should vary drastically depending upon who I am to meet. Not true.

Yes, I always try to present myself in an acceptable manner relative to the seasonal weather conditions. Whether I am dressed in slacks and a sweater or clean jeans and a "personalized" pet-sitting t-shirt, I always know beforehand if I will be encountering "stranger-friendly" pets, jumping dogs or shy felines.

On several occasions, I have been surprised to learn from these new clients that the sitter they used previously or the sitting service they turned down had arrived so neatly attired that the *client* felt underdressed. Clients have shared their concerns with me that these sitters looked unapproachable. Their nails too long, too perfectly manicured, not a hair out of place or a wrinkle in their clothes! "I have to wonder if she would even sit on the floor to play with Sparky," I've been told. What if Gomer jumps up and rips her blouse? Will she get mad and push him away?"

So you see, as a professional pet sitter, a happy medium must be attained. A professional appearance (and attitude) certainly is important. It is also somewhat of an opinion, as to how we "look" or present ourselves. What is acceptable to one client, may not be presentable to the next. The doctor or office executive (without human children of his/her own) may want to be assured through visual means that you are not *so professional* that you wouldn't get down on your hand and knees to play peek-a-boo with Sassy. Just like the beach-bum-store-clerk may not want to see a sitter as unkempt as he may be.

Good judgment and common sense is always the best guide. I simply wanted to pass along another experienced viewpoint for that imperative initial meeting. I commend Kate Barclay of *Kozy Kritters* for a well-written and sensible article.

Hiring Employees: Easier Than You Think!

by Cynthia Elkey, Rover's Recess Inc., Charlottesville, VA

August 1995, Vol. II, Issue 3

Invariably, after being in the pet sitting business for awhile, we come to the crossroads of whether or not to keep our companies small and continue to do all the pet sitting ourselves, or to hire some people to help us. This is a very personal decision, and not one to be taken lightly. If you decide to hire people, then you need to decide if you should hire them as independent contractors or employees. This seems to be the hottest issue in our industry!

The purpose of this article is not to debate the issue of whether to have employees or independent contractors. I will say though, that in making my decision to hire pet sitters as employees, it was a question of how much loyalty and control that I wanted. I wanted pet sitters who would only work for my company, and I wanted to be able to direct and evaluate their job performance. So, since I desired loyalty and control, having employees seemed like the only way to go! Also, call me chicken if you like, but I never wanted to have to deal with the Internal Revenue Service (IRS) if there should ever be a question to arise as to the status of the people who work for me.

What I want to let you know is that if you do go the employee route, it's not that hard to do! My experience and research has shown there is approximately a 10% to 12% cost to a company for taxes and insurance which you need to consider when setting your prices for your clients and your salary for your employees. As far as paying insurance, the insurance companies will determine what you need to pay them and then they will bill you. As far as taxes go, it's just a matter of knowing which taxes to pay and when. You're probably already very organized and disciplined in following a pet-sitting schedule, so now you simply add a few more dates and deadlines to your schedule book so that you'll pay your taxes on time and avoid paying penalties. Just as you wouldn't forget to visit a pet, you won't forget to make your tax payments!

As an employer, you'll be responsible for federal taxes and probably some state taxes. For federal taxes, contact the IRS and request a copy of Circular E, Employer's Tax Guide. You will also need to obtain an SS-4 form so that you can apply for a federal identification number for your company. W-4 forms will also be needed so that your employees can fill them out to declare their filing status and any exemptions. The IRS Tax Guide will tell you how much in tax to withhold from your employee's paycheck according to the number of exemptions they have claimed. It will also tell you how much Social Security (6.2%) to withhold and how much Medicare (1.45%) to withhold. (Your company must match the Social Security and Medicare costs.) The employer is also liable for federal unemployment taxes (FUTA) which is .8%, making your total federal tax liability 8.45% (multiply .0845 times total payroll.) The Tax Guide will tell you when and where to make these tax deposits.

State and local taxes will vary, and you will need to contact each appropriate tax department to find out what your tax liability is with them. In the state of Virginia where my business is located, my company pays a Virginia Unemployment Tax, and then the county in which we operate requires a payroll tax for us to have a business license. The city where we are located does not have a payroll tax. Be aware though that my situation is not the case everywhere - some larger cities require a local withholding tax and also require the outright purchase of a city/county privilege (business) license on an annual basis. Each state does have an unemployment tax, though, and most require a state identification number. Contact the appropriate office in your state for details and correct filing forms.

Another cost to your company for employees is that of worker's compensation insurance. In many states this is required whether you have employees or independent contractors. Be sure to check with your state government for the regulations that apply. The cost for this coverage may vary from state to state. In Virginia, my company pays 1.91% (multiply .0191 times total payroll).

You will also need to notify your liability insurance company when you hire people, as your cost may be contingent upon payroll totals. Each insurance company may be different from the next, so it's important that your insurance company knows that you have people working for you. You don't want to take the risk of their not being covered under your policy. The insurance policy offered through PSI is probably the best insurance to have because it is finely tuned to pet sitting and is very affordable.

Once you have people working for you, you will also need to get a dishonesty bond. Basically, the way a dishonesty bond works is that the company that issues you a dishonesty bond acts like a bank guarantee for the amount of the bond. That is, if it's proven in a court of law that one of your employees or independent contractors steals something from a client and the item cannot be recovered, then the insurance (bonding) company will pay your client the value of the item, up to the value of your bond. Then, your company must pay back the insurance company (probably at a high interest rate!) The cost of a dishonesty bond is minimal, and, in all honesty, your clients want to know that you're bonded, even if they don't have any idea exactly what bonding is!

The following is an approximate percentage of payroll that my company pays in taxes and insurance per year:

Social Security	6.20	%
Medicare	1.45	%
FUTA	0.80	%
State Unemployment	0.0018	%
Worker's Comp.	1.90	%
Liability & Bonding	0.001	% (approx.)
Total Tax & Ins. Cost	10.35	%

The federal taxes will be the same for your company, but the state and local taxes and insurance costs will vary. You can anticipate employer costs of 10% - 15% to cover this expense, so simply add $1-$2 per visit to your pet sitting rates!

One important thing to remember is not to be intimidated by all this tax and insurance business. It's simple to do once you have it all in place. And, you can always get free advice from the IRS, or you can simplify the process even more by utilizing a good accountant. It's really just a matter of learning what you must pay and when - and then remembering to pay it on time! It's no big deal - really!

Love Me, Love My Dog Sitting... ...and Please Pay A Reasonable Rate For It Too!

By Amy Brodsky, Dog Sitting, Middletown, NY

March/April 1999, Vol. IV, Issue 2

After returning from the PSI cruise convention, I realized just how very hard we as pet sitters are working. We deserve a raise! We're working a long span of hours from early morning to late at night. We are doing business on weekends and holidays! Any other business that works these hours charges accordingly. I know that dogs and other pets are great fun and are all so cute to watch, but it is still a business. I started out at $12 a visit in my upstate New York town. After two of my friends watched me pet sit, they notified me of the following: three dogs jumping and lunging at me (I was new) broke down to $4 a dog or .50 cents per jump! I decided then that I had to raise my rates. It's now three years later and my rates are still going up depending upon the job. When I charge the right price, I feel better about being in this profession. Here are some tips to help you treat your business as a serious venture:

- First, sell yourself on you! If you offer outstanding service, believe it and let it add to your confidence when talking to prospects. Offer letters of recommendation.

- Understand that you have a service that people want and need. At the convention, I heard so many sitters say that when they quote their rates to prospects, the prospect says "the kennel is so much less." If they are calling you, they obviously want to hear about why your service is better. Take the time, calmly rather than defensively, to state the benefits. Comfort, less stress, convenience, less health risk, and your love are some of the benefits you should be discussing to sell the service you provide. If you sell this well, the price will be a mere factor!

- Create rapport. Clients buy from people they like. Take the time to have a conversation. Let the customer talk then listen, listen, listen.

- Listen to your customers' needs by asking the right questions. What kind of pets do you have? What are their names? How have they been cared for in the past? Were you happy with that method? These are questions that will allow the prospect to sell himself on your service. Think about it - how often have you heard the story of the relative that forgot about someone's pet, or the time Rover threw up for one week after the kennel stay?

People will pay for better service as long as the job is done well. Most of us are very passionate about pets and our careers. To keep us in this profession, we need to be financially rewarded for our efforts! Let's help ourselves and the industry as a whole by equitably charging for the valuable service we provide.

Pet Sitting Safety

Summer 1996 Vol. III, Issue 3

"If I'm concerned about my own safety, I usually call a friend. This phone call indicated my arrival time, where I am meeting, the phone number, name of person I'm meeting and expected meeting duration. Immediately upon completion of the meeting I call my friend to advise that I am okay and add a thank you."

" I give my staff pagers and we have emergency codes. So, if they need to contact me they call my pager and put in their emergency code. I know to call them immediately. If I need them, I call their pagers."

"I supply personal alarms for my sitters and myself. They are available at any "dollar" store for about $3-5. Insert batteries, pull the alarm pin, and a loud noise sounds. The alarm comes in handy if you encounter a very curious dog while walking client dogs as the noise will scare the dog away."

"I have Caller ID, so when my sitters call me it is programmed for the time and which customer house they call came from. This helps me to keep accurate time sheets of each sitter as well. And, my sitters feel more comfortable just knowing that they have to call in."

"Familiarize yourself with the areas in which you provide sitting services. Know safe routes for dog walking, the location of police/fire departments, stores with late hours, etc."

"Keep your car in good running condition with your gas tank filled. Remember to lock your car doors while driving and while parked at client homes."

"Leave an outside light on (or ask clients to use timers) so that evening pet care visits don't have to be made in the dark."

"Have house or car key in hand and ready to use when arriving/departing during your pet sitting rounds."

Reader Survey:
Saying "No" Experiences to Share

November 1994, Vol. 1, Issue 3

We never accept cat jobs where the owner wants service every three days. If every other day, we add $1.00 to the basic charge. It's not fair to the kitties!

I say no to the person looking for a "bargain" price, the sharing arrangement and to the extremely dirty house!

I say no when they expect me to pay because their dog chewed up something-no, no, no!

I said no when asked to sit for a wolf dog.

I have started telling clients to get rid of fleas or I won't sit again! We will not visit cats less than once daily because of the rapid course of various illnesses, such as urinary blockages. It feels great to say "no" to last minute new clients. Three years ago we said "yes" to everyone!

Plowing and Snow Shoveling

Fall 1996, Vol. III, Issue 4

Last Quarter's Question:
"For my colleagues in the north: I am interested in the different approaches you may have used during the winter months with respect to plowing and snow shoveling while providing care to vacationing clients. As many of you know, last year was quite harsh and I found myself digging out paths to my clients' homes. I have a few ideas for amending my contract, but I was wondering if any of you applied additional charges for these services, or if you applied an across-the-board increase to all your fees during this season. Thanks for you help."

...I ask that my pet sitters in Colorado and Montana at least shovel the entry for customers. We do not charge extra, but we hope that customers are so appreciative of this extra effort that they will tip the pet sitter. We do always ask who to contact for snowplowing during winter months. The customer leaves a check in advance or contacts the plower in advance.

...I don't live in the North, but in the South where plants need watering on hot days, I charge extra for anything that is not in a plant pot. Yards, gardens, etc., are prorated depending on the amount of time it takes to water them. All based on $12.00 for every 1/2 hour - 30 minutes. But yes, I would charge for snowstorms.

...I don't shovel for my clients. If people do, I think they should charge accordingly—if agreed to, in advance, by clients.

...Make arrangements ahead of time. I would not do the plowing because if an injury occurs, they might not have homeowner's coverage, you might lose work performance, etc. Stick to the basics of taking care of animals, mail and house inspection. Also, if there are hurricanes or tornadoes in the area, have arrangements with a tree removal service in advance. Always check with owners first, however. As the season wore on, I began to add a standard question when doing the interview and contract. "Do you have a contract with a snow removal company, and if not, and we can't get to your house, do we have your permission to contract one if needed?" I never got a "No" answer, and I merely hand-wrote it into the contract. I service a rural area; many homes have mile-long drives, so there is no way I could handle snow removal myself. I simply made it clear (gently, kindly and professionally) that this was the responsibility of the client.

Pet-Sitting Supplies

March/April 1997, Vol. IV Issue 2

The Jan/Feb WORLD "Question of the Issue" asked how colleagues handle customers who don't leave enough food or supplies - especially clients who seem to be making a habit of this practice! Here's what members had to say on the subject:

...My service contract has an additional hourly and mileage charge for shopping.

...I **tell** the customers to have enough on hand! If you have to buy products, present receipts with your statement. Don't forget about these extra expenses!

...My contract specifically states the client is responsible for food, supplies and cost of delivery.

...I call the client in advance to confirm upcoming reservations and remind them to have ample food/supplies on hand!

...The client pays an extra visit fee for having the sitter go to the store for food, plus the client reimburses the sitter for costs of product. I have never had a client complain.

...I charge a $10.00 surcharge plus the cost of food or supplies.

...I dropped a customer just recently who had been with me for three years for doing this once too often!

...I leave a "checklist" with clients of things they need to do/have on hand before leaving - this way there are no excuses except for in cases of emergency!

...We always collect an advance deposit ($25 minimum or 1/2 of overnight fees) and then use this if anything has to be purchased for the pet/home. Receipts are kept so we can later bill the customer. Also, we charge them a $2.00 service fee plus mileage for our shopping trip.

...A new client did not leave enough cottage cheese for her dog. I bought a container, and she was so grateful. The lost cost didn't set me back, and she's sent many referrals as well as tipped me well.

The Up and Downside of Pet Sitting

by Clairce J. Pugh, Whiskers, Wings and Other Things

March/April 1999, Vol. IV, Issue 2

I smiled to myself complacently as the young girl backed away from me. Her mother, obviously certain that she could help me avoid further embarrassment (like when your slip is showing and nobody tells you), whispered, "Excuse me, but you have some bird dirt kind of running down the back of your blouse." I looked her right in the eye and replied, "No, that's horse drool. There's bird poo on the other shoulder though." And I turned back in line as I waited to be checked out with my bread and milk purchase. It was the end of my afternoon calls, and I was looking forward to a hot cup of tea—and to change my blouse.

Being a pet sitter requires a total change of attitude on one's part, and a total overhaul of one's personality where self-esteem is concerned.
People often tell us, "You two have such a marvelous way with animals. They can hardly resist you."

"That's because we usually stink," I reply, while my daughter/ business partner, Carol, stands there with a twinkle in her eye. "Animals love it when they can smell other animals on your clothes and hands," she says. "The smellier, the better."

People back away from us in horror. Only our clients love us as we are. And the Lord, of course. After all, He gave the first pet sitting assignment. He must have known what it would involve.

I spent years being a refined person. And I was pretty good at it, as far as my bank account would allow. I had taught Released Time Christian Education in California for several years. We were always reminded that wherever we went in public; somebody would recognize us and the example we set was of great importance. I worked as an administrative secretary prior to my pet sitting career, and I wore beautiful blouses, skirts, hosiery and heels to work every day. It was an extreme act of courage on my part not to wear makeup for major surgery. I play classical piano (the easier pieces and arrangements) and play the piano for church services. I was always clean, neat, well made up and attractively dressed. My hair was sprayed into place and didn't dare move.

You know where this is leading, don't you? Makeup lasts only part way through the first pet call of the day. Perspiration has you looking like a striped, multicolored zebra in short order. Hair is something birds try to rearrange while we reach into their cages to clean them, or something horses can grab hold of and pull while you're trying to fill their watering trough. Puppies get excited and tinkle, just a little bit, as soon as you pick them up, and cat hair sticks to everything except blue jeans. By the time you've finished just a few pet calls, you can easily look like a female big foot with a most interesting coat of fur. Our own dogs can't wait for us to get home so they can sniff all the critters we've cared for second hand. In addition, they sniff out any remnants of puperoni or kitty salmon treats now crumbled in our pockets. Avon never came up with a sniffer's delight such as we.

The benefits, you ask? All over this countryside, dogs will spring to our defense to protect our endless pocket of treats. We save lots of money on makeup. In preparing our financial portfolios, we now know the steady growth in such products as those made by Scott Towel and Land's End Clothing. These are absolutely essential for the pet sitter who intends to survive. As the pet sitting industry grows, so does the stock in markets such as those mentioned. The more we encounter pups that show their displeasure of owners being gone by developing diarrhea, the more we know to invest in Scott Towels.

Living in what is referred to as the "high country" in Tennessee, and coming from some nice flat driving lanes as those in central Florida, as Carol drove, I rode around this countryside with my mouth gaping open. "I am definitely not going to drive up a driveway when all I can see at the end of that driveway is the top of a play gym set!" Thus, I established my limits, and mentally noted homes unacceptable as prospective clients. Well, that would limit us to about five clients. Not good. Had to rethink that one. Benefit: enhanced driving skills and a daily workout on nerve control.

I don't have to feel self-conscious when my arthritis causes me to limp, as I have several fuzzy clients who limp also. Old dogs, old cats and I have a lot in common. Even to our sometimes grumpy attitudes. I can talk to them, and they understand. I'm much more inclined to be understanding with them when they're grumpy, and I don't take it as a personal affront. Benefit: grumpy animals cause me to stop and think that everyone, people too, can have bad days. Be a little more understanding— nothing personal intended.

One also becomes more adept at identifying honesty and genuine animal skills in others. The other day one of the morning shows on television had a gentlemen demonstrate—on a real honest to goodness live cat—how to give a cat a pill. First, he picked it up by the scruff of its neck, "like the mother cat does". Then he placed it on a towel on a slippery table (supposedly getting it off "familiar terrain and keeping it from getting a solid foothold on fabric"). He proceeded to gently pull the cat's head back so there was a smooth, straight neckline. He gently opened its mouth and popped in a pill. Either that cat was high on drugs or it was an amazing lifelike puppet. What he did not show was actuality. The cat hiding under the very middle of a king sized bed or in the darkest depths of a closet. The enormous, earth shattering shriek if you dare to move an arm and hand in the feline's direction. The hissing and snarling you endure, warning of unbelievable pain if you even dare try to administer a pill. The fact that all cats can get an excellent foothold on a steel surface covered with two inches of grease, and that all the towel will serve to do is provide kitty with material to bind two of its paws, claws extended and sunk deep into your arm, securely in place. Opening the cat's mouth with your one remaining serviceable hand reveals fangs meant to rip and shred. The sounds uttered from an angry cat's throat defy description, but there is a reason the same sound is used in all horror films. If you coat the pill with butter, it will make your helpless fingers taste better to kitty, while the pill slips out of its mouth. Any second attempt is met with graver danger. Your life will be on the line with a third try. Thus, I learned to take television shows with a grain of salt and a sense of humor. Everyone needs at least one laugh a day. I'll call PSI for information on how to best give a cat a pill. Working with Carol, we take turns being the "bad guy and the good guy" and spend a portion of our salary and free time making catnip pillows as bribes.

And finally, one of the greatest benefits is that you learn you can change your lifestyle, develop a sense of humor and discover that you are a terrific person because your furry friends have identified you as such. Their instincts and wisdom are something to be trusted and admired. Welcome to the club.

From Pet Sitting I've Learned...

May/June 1999, Vol. IV. Issue 3.

Smile - Enjoy pets, people and your job - every day!
P. Hunter, Furry Critters, Newport, NC

Keep your eye on the time when making rounds! It's fun to stay and play, but move on when the time is up and go on with the day!
Susan Arnold, Pet Service, North Hampton, PA

There is never a boring day. You learn something new all the time. You really need to be an animal lover to do it, and there is not a lot of free time.
Dawn's Tender Care, Glen Arbor, MI

Keep the client's house keys on you once you enter the house until you lock the door to leave. *Anonymous*

Some days you step in it and some days you don't! Sunshine days and little cold noses are all it takes to make my day!
Candy's Pampered Pets, Hayward, CA

The longer the pet sitting period, the less likely the owners are to leave enough food and supplies. *Deb Carroll, Pet Playmates, Bradenton, FL*

Be patient with new clients. They don't always understand what is needed for the proper care of their home and pets. Walk them through it slowly and thoroughly. *Home and Pet Nanny Service, Seattle, WA*

I've learned that my clients, who dearly love their pets, will be much, much cleaner with their pets' food and water bowls on my second gig to their home. It makes me feel good that my washing bowls every day has made them more aware. *Sue Uhl, Daisy Dew Pet Sitters, Sparta, NC*

Not only are there only two paper towel sheets left, usually there is no toilet paper. *Nancy Watson, The Cat Nanny, Indianapolis, IN*

I've learned that clients think you know everything about pet sitting and animals. *Leslie Kaufman, On All Fours, Manhattan, NY*

I've learned that pet sitting is full of surprises. The job will never be as easy as you think. *TLC Pet Care, Yucca Valley, CA*

Appear professional and organized because the British are suspicious. References from previous customers are critical.
S. Cringle, Sheena's Pet Service, Derbys, England

No matter how much reminding you do for customers to book early, there will always be the last minute frantic phone call.
Personal Care Pet Sitting, Womelsdorf, PA

Always act as though you're being watched. *Anonymous, Houston, TX*

Expect the unexpected. *Sherri's Furry Friends, LTD. Dublin, OH*

Winning the affection of a shy or fearful pet is one of the most rewarding parts of my job.
Kellie Brashears, Happy At Home Pet Sitting, Abingdon, MD

If you wait until the last visit to completely "clean-up," the clients will come home before the last visit.
R. Bovello, Gaithersburg Pet Sitting, Gaithersburg, MD

I am truly happy. All of my pets make me feel so loved, wanted and needed —It's wonderful! *Linda's Pet Sitting*

PSI Membership is the best advertisement - it means a lot to clients.
Lorrie Gallagher, Puppy Love, San Francisco, CA

Schedule one week of vacation yearly, and take off one day a week.
Jody Issod, Puss & Boots Pet Sitting, Marlboro, MA

The best way is to treat others' pets as you do your own. *Krista Stabell, The Always Pampered Pet, College Station, TX*

I've learned that I love this job more than I ever thought I would.
Anonymous

Do not leave lamps, especially halogen ones, on. Pets can knock them over. Instead, leave on overhead lights or a light above the stove.
Nancy Brooks, Spoil-Me-Rotten Animal Care, Oak Ridge, NC

Never try to give advice about raising animals to someone who already thinks their way is best. *Anonymous*

That pets are even more precocious, precious, and perceptive than I ever thought possible. *Anonymous*

I've learned that the client's friends, neighbors, and relatives who some-times "help" almost never do their "favor" as well as we do our job.
G. Zimmerman, Precious Pets Pet Sitting Service, Sinking Spring, PA

Pets are better than a classroom of thirteen-year olds!
Cindy Ersek, Teacher's Pets, Concordville, PA

Never leave home without a Milk Bone and a leash!
Stephanie Clark, The Pampered Pet, Pittsboro, NC

When a client calls and says, "No need to call back unless there is a problem," what they really mean is, "Call back immediately or I will phone you at 11 p.m. in a panic." *Anonymous*

I've learned that the number of minutes you have to fly across town to get to the next visit is directly proportional to the minimal speeds of the car in front of you and the distance from your bumper to the car tailgating you.
G. Zimmerman, Precious Pets Pet Sitting Service, Sinking Spring, PA

Don't be afraid to say NO to an arrogant client that is going to give you a hard time before the service has even started - that's a red flag.
Janice Ash, Clermont, FL

I've learned that I have a lot more to learn!
Anonymous, Spokane, WA

People that own pets and care enough to use a pet sitter are usually just as great as their pets.
Pam Brown, Personalized Pet Sitting Service, Marietta, GA

Pets even welcome you in your PJs - clothes over of course!
Bone Voyage Home Pet Care, Macedon, NY

How attached pets become to you as their special friend.
Sylvia Koczerzuk, Walkabout Services, Windsor, Ontario, Canada

The Good Buddies Home Pet Care's Top Ten List of "You Know You're a Pet Sitter When..."

by Claire Newick AHT, Good Buddies Home Pet Care

Fall 1996, Vol. III, Issue 4

10. Every time you reach into a jacket or pants pocket you pull out a poop bag.

9. By the end of the day, you're ready to talk to someone who will talk back to you.

8. If someone tells you, "I wish I had your job" one more time, you'll tell them that some days you would give it to them and be on the next plane to Tahiti.

7. Pet sitting is the first thing you think about when you wake up in the morning and the last thing you think about before drifting off to sleep at night.

6. You wonder where the really fun places are to vacation in February and October.

5. You go to the bank and see that it's closed because of a holiday, and you don't have the slightest idea what holiday it is.

4. You constantly walk around with animal hair all over your clothes, and you wouldn't dare wear anything not machine washable.

3. You don't get excited because it's Friday, but, then again, you don't get bummed because it's Monday.

2. After a full day of walking dogs, it feels like your arms are longer than everyone else's.

1. When your friends call you up and suggest going somewhere, you respond, "Only if you're driving."

Eloise Trosan, CityPet, Philadelphia, PA, has been pet sitting for more than 20 years and has been a PSI member since 1995. In 1997, she began a regular column in *The WORLD* called "Sitter to Sitter." During the course of its run, Eloise dispensed wisdom tinged with gentle humor to every PSI member who opened the pages of the magazine.

Speaking "from the trenches," Eloise was an authoritative voice who was certain to help any pet sitter who listened.

The Sitter to Sitter Series: Eloise Trosan

Sitter to Sitter: The Good News Is....

by Eloise I. Trosan, City Pet, Pittsburgh, PA

Jan/Feb 1997, Vol. IV, Issue 1

I barely noticed that beautiful, early summer day several years ago in mid-June. Too busy, I came home that afternoon from the morning pet sitting to a bunch of messages on my answering machine. Sigh. I was already tired and summer had barely started. I sat back in my office chair and had to seriously and fully admit that my little pet sitting business had run amok. I sadly acknowledged how truly exhausted I was, and how out of touch with my family and friends I had become. I was the one who was always late, couldn't go, had to work, etc. I was "burned out" and wondered how it had come to this.

Since 1984, I had worked so hard to build this business and had overcome so many obstacles. I was almost too tired to examine problems. However, a look at the boring, low-paying jobs in the "Classifieds" was enough to make me focus my last irritated nerve ending to try to save the unusual job that I still loved. I really began to examine what was wrong. I picked apart our procedures and style, brain-stormed with my best employee and hunted down another pet sitter to talk to.

What was the biggest problem? My schedule. I was pet sitting night and day, every day, to almost the exclusion of everything else. I was up early and out late almost every day, I was tired all the time. I worked 7 days a week, all holidays and all weekends, driving a ridiculous number of miles. How long can someone do this? Why was I doing so much? Why was it so hard to get work turned over to employees? I had four of them by then. Why was more help not "more help?" I had customers who wanted visits that were so specialized in terms of timing and procedures that I was losing money and time. Other businesses had rules, procedures, policies and hours. Mine was like Topsie in *Uncle Tom's Cabin* who "just growed." My baby had grown into a monster.

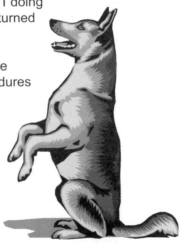

Would the world come to an end if I said NO to a customer? Would it end if I put a limit on the size of our customer base? Would it end if I offered services to a smaller area? If the services were more defined? If I asked customers for more cooperation? Would I lose the whole business in the end? Almost ready to quit, I was losing it now anyway.

I have, since then, talked and listened to many other sitters. I've found that many of us have fallen into some of the same traps. We gave away our services too cheaply. We drove too far. We did too much. We promised too much. We tried to please everyone, even at our own great expense, had unrealistic expectations, or worse, we didn't project into the future at all. We failed to communicate with our customers, and our customers ended up running our businesses by default. We lacked rules and protocol. We were afraid to say, "NO!" We were tired as hell.

The good news is that the above problems are solvable to a reasonable degree. This is the beginning of a series of articles that will suggest possible detailed ways to get some serious professional control over our pet sitting businesses so that we own them at least a little bit more than they own us. Some of the procedures are things that other sitters do. Nothing is carved in stone. There are as many configurations as there are sitters. So, this series is meant to be an " a la carte" experience. I hope you find some of the inventive ways discussed are of use to you.

Sitter to Sitter: Help!

by Eloise I. Trosan

May/June 1997, Vol. IV Issue 3

Help! Sooner or later, most sitters feel in need of help. Holidays or summers that are too busy, time off and working almost every weekend non-stop eventually take their toll. Right after screaming for help, comes "decisions, decisions."

It is a testament to creativity to see the various ways that sitters solve this problem. There seem to be as many ways as there are sitters. This makes sense because the variables sitters face are so many that each has to analyze his or her own situation to come up with a way that will work. Here is rundown of just a few of the common ways that sitters get help.

Sitters who decide not to hire help at all. Some sitters just decide they don't want the bother of hiring help. The forms and legal aspects of hiring employees or I.C.'s are just more than they care to deal with. Happy with their businesses as they are, they put a cap on their customer base and only take new customers to make up for natural attrition. When they book up for busy times, they refer work out to other area sitters or simply inform customers that they are booked to capacity.

Sitters who hire limited help. Some sitters hire limited help in the form of one or two people who don't work all the time. They take work off the owners' hands when the owner gets overloaded, or take over when the owners need some time off or want a vacation. Usually, some sort of percentage is taken by the owner on these jobs. While it is unlikely that the owner will make real profit on this kind of help, it is usually possible to break even, reduce the work load for the owner and keep these customers calling back at slower times when the owner can handle them. These hired helpers can also be used as backup if the owner has a crisis situation come up. After all, we get sick too and have our own family emergencies sometimes.

Sitters who hire lots of help. Some sitters become sitting companies. They hire anywhere from a half dozen to as many as 30 or more sitters to work for them. The volume of work that can be taken is much greater, of course, and since a percentage goes to the owner, the more volume there is, the more likely that profit will be the result for these companies. The owner's role as pet sitter, depending on how big these operations get, varies from still doing a great deal of the actual pet sitting to being a full-time manager of people who pet sit.

Sitter to Sitter: If it was in her calendar, why wasn't it in mine?

by Eloise I. Trosan

March/April 1997 Vol IV Issue 2

I dropped by a customer's house one August evening to pick up keys. I was just about to send out a newsletter informing customers that I would be out of town in mid-October, so while I was there, I told her about it. She immediately ran to her calendar and saw that she had dates blocked off for a trip for which they had airline and hotel reservations already made. She heaved a sigh of relief. Her trip was the week before mine. This customer, a chronic short-notice caller, is representative of one of my biggest problems. If those reservations were already made, the dates already in her calendar, why weren't they in my calendar? When was she going to call me? Three days before they were leaving? I didn't say anything to her at that time.

I took the dates to put in my calendar, but I knew immediately what I was going to do. This continual short-notice problem was a big one, and the first one I had to tackle. This was the primary reason that hiring help was not "more help". With too much short notice, there was not time to distribute work. Distributing work is work. It takes time. I had to ask my customers for more cooperation to keep this business, with a full, active customer base of almost 250, functioning in a more efficient way.

So, out went an almost personal letter to all my current customers. The letter explained that the business was going well and that we loved our jobs, but that we were experiencing a crisis because of too many short-notice calls. It was not a letter of blame. We asked for their help. The letter explained that we were aware that customers did not really understand how seven day-a-week businesses like this operated. We told them that we just wanted to fill them in on a few things so that we could maintain availability for them and some sanity for us. The letter explained that we never advertised this as an emergency or on-call service, but that somehow it had become one by default. We simply asked that those customers who knew when they were going away and were making reservations for planes and hotels not to forget about us. We reminded them we had a number of emergencies to deal with for customers, and that we tried to accommodate those who leave more spontaneously as well. We pointed out that, if we knew the jobs were already planned, we could plan more efficiently and increase our availability.

The response was wonderful. People understood completely and immediately began making reservations for all trips that were planned in advance. It was a tremendous relief for us. Work could be distributed, and I could plan personal things and get some much needed time off.

Many sitters have business hours—designed daily hours during which they will receive or return phone calls. It is difficult for sitters to end their days. Most of us are out caring for dogs at least well into the early part of the evening. Phone answering and call returning ends for many sitters around 7 or 8 p.m. so that sitters can have time with their own families and time to wind down before starting early for another busy day. Most calls that come later in the evening are routine reservations, check-ins or inquiries. The occasional emergency can be dealt with, if necessary, the rest can wait without harm until the next day's business hours. Your customer should have all your procedures, hours and expectations in writing so that they understand what their responsibility is going to be.

In the next column, I will write about the ways that sitters make decisions about whether or not to hire help, and when they do, how they distribute work to employees.

Some regular features and columns in *The WORLD* lasted for only a short time, while others that debuted in the early years are still around today. "Bright Ideas" is one of those that endured.

"Bright Ideas" provides a way for all PSI members to share tips with one another. Business tips, pet care tips, marketing tips and more—you can find it all underneath the trademark light bulb of "Bright Ideas."

Bright Ideas

First "Bright Ideas"

August 1994, Vol. 1, Issue 2

I made it a practice of scanning the weekly business page in our local newspaper that listed area promotions, new hires, awards, etc. If I recognized a name that I knew to be a client, I always sent a congratulations card on behalf of the company.

For newcomers who had obviously moved from another locale, according to the paper, I sent a card welcoming them to our area and enclosed a "Try Us, You'll Like Us" coupon for a free pet-sitting visit. I mailed these to their places of employment and they did result in new business for us!
—*Patti Moran, Pet Sitters International*

Make sure you know where the client's phone book is located. The one visit where I failed to take my list of emergency veterinary phone numbers, wouldn't you know it, I had a sick dog. It was frustrating to not know where to begin to look for the phone book! So, preferably keep your own list of emergency phone numbers handy, but also ask the client where you would find the phone book if needed!
—Eleanor Caldwell, Crazy 'Bout Critters

February 1995, Vol. II, Issue 1

We have a section in our company's newsletter called "Favorite Customer Comments." In this column we share the ego-boosting notes we receive with customer payments or those jotted on our Sitter Evaluation Forms. To see their comments "in print" lets the client know we do read and appreciate the wonderful things they say to us, shows other customers that some clients are just crazy about us, and hopefully inspires customers to let us know what they think about our services.
—*Patti Corlin, Pet Sitters Plus All The Trimmings*

May 1995, Vol. II, Issue 2

- I have just started advertising the fact that I offer free rentals from a selection of pet-related books and videos that I own.

- If you use a client's toilet (lots of coffee in the morning!) be sure it's through running before you leave. Two of my clients had faulty toilets and I didn't know it. It's a good thing I waited before I left!

- Never discuss travel plans over cellular or cordless phones as they might be monitored or overheard on other cordless phones in the neighborhood or on scanner radio frequencies.

February 1996, Vol III, Issue 1

In a recent company newsletter, I suggested to clients that if they have good quality, unused produce, baked goods, or dairy products that may go to waste during their upcoming trip, they could leave them as a "tip" for their pet sitter. After all, food is too expensive to waste these days. Although I wasn't sure if the clients would be receptive to this idea, I have heard several nice comments from customers about this suggestion and several clients have left perishable items for their sitter. Waste not, want not!
Karen Herbig, Home Pet Care Services

When putting up posters around town, attach pull off tags with your phone number so interested people can take your phone number with them. If they have to pull out a pen and paper, they may decide it's too much trouble, or, when ready to call you, they may confuse you with a competitor when looking up your name and phone number in the Yellow Pages.
Reader Survey Contributor

May 1996 Vol. III Issue 2

I printed the word "IDENTIFICATION" on my PSI membership card and then punched a hole through it and inserted a chain so I could wear it around my neck when visiting clients. It looks very professional, like utility company employees wear! People like to see ID before letting anyone into their home, so this allows me to provide identification as well as to tout my PSI membership!
David Weiner, Mister Pet In-Home Pet Sitting, New Jersey

For animals that try to escape through the front door when I am trying to enter, I shake a plastic market bag and they usually run back.
Marty Kirkland, Critter Sitters, California

I clip pet food coupons and leave them at the client's home who uses that particular food. Clients appreciate this courtesy and it doesn't cost my business anything!
Reader Survey

Your Holiday Gift Ideas

Summer 1996, Vol. 3, Issue 3

 In the Fall '95 *WORLD*, we asked members for gift idea suggestions for veterinarians, groomers, clients etc. Since the holidays will be here before we know it, we wanted to share member ideas with you now, so you can do your holiday shopping and planning early!

- Send fruit baskets
- Subscriptions to *Dog Fancy* and/or *Cat Fancy* (Use the PSI discount on subscriptions!)
- Gift certificate to a favorite restaurant
- Candles and homemade cookies shaped like cats, dogs, bones
- Handmade ornaments (pasta angels, cinnamon applesauce bears, etc.) Ed. Note: Would whoever contributed this idea send us more "how-to" details? Photos with instructions, recipes?
- I prefer to give gifts at another time of the year when they don't "get lost"!
- Baskets filled with healthy goodies
- Pizza gift certificate for the office
- A big calendar for the office with my company's name and phone number on it!
- Cheese tray
- I send a holiday card with my company magnet in it. All vets and clients have refrigerators!

- Garland or wreath with animal décor with card attached Ed. Note: Please send photo and/or instructions
- Large popcorn tin
- Holiday donuts
- Bookmark
- I make gift bags/stockings with toys, chews, canned food etc. and put the pet's name on it
- Quilted appliquéd dog/cat tree
- Ornament of customer's breed
- I take all of my sitters out to dinner

Summer 1996, Vol. III, Issue 3

Several months ago I put several of my high-income producing clients on a retainer fee. The client will pay for a three to six month period up front (usually $250 for three months and $500 for six months), and I keep a running tab for the services rendered. At the end of each quarter, I present the client with a current retainer statement. This system gives me more cash flow, prevents the client from having to write as many checks, and it means I don't have to worry about collecting for each job!

Alice S. Wilson, Williamsburg Pet & House Sitting

I ring the doorbell before entering homes just in case the client has unexpectedly arrived home early, but mostly to notify pets I'm there and entering. They are always there to greet me! I also (in non-residential areas where it won't disturb neighbors) lightly honk my horn to bring in horses, livestock and dogs for feeding and care. They know the sound of my horn and come running.

Reader Survey Idea

One of my clients has a spare key attached to the end of her dog leash to protect herself from lock outs-a good idea to share with dog owners!

Reader Survey Idea

Make keys work like new with the help of a lead pencil. Rubbing the pencil on the teeth of the key acts as a non-greasy lubricant to make it work more smoothly. Keep a lead pencil in your Survival Bag for "ornery" keys! (Works on zippers too!)

Reader Survey Idea

Fall 1996, Vol. III, Issue 4

In my spare time, I help distribute a monthly publication in which I advertise to help defray the cost of the advertisement.

To temporarily stop a dog from digging: While filling the hole, put some "doo" from the dog's pen up near the top of the fill. Cover it with a little dirt. A dog will not dig into its own feces. The dog may choose a new location. Repeat as needed.

Jan/Feb 1997 Vol IV, Issue 1

All the pet sitters from Home Pet Care in our two locations (soon to be three) wear smocks in our color, royal blue, embroidered with our company name and logo. Because I am a veterinary microbiologist, I am used to wearing a smock while working with animals. Not all of my pet sitters are accustomed to a work smock, so I try to encourage them to wear it and wear it with pride. The following is list of reasons why they should wear their smocks. I hope you think they are all "Bright Ideas!"

Reasons to wear your smock:

- Identifies you immediately as a Home Pet Care pet sitter. Sets us apart from other pet-sitting services.

- It is the one constant for the animals if or when a change in pet sitter occurs. A dog is more likely to let you enter its territory if it recognizes something about you.

- For difficult or older animals, it helps them identify you immediately— no confusion for them. You will appear the same to them and not different due to different clothing.

- Helps prevent the spread of diseases to your own animals and between households. It can be removed before entering your own home.

- Identifies you immediately as a service provider to neighbors and law officials.

- Veterinarians and staff will recognize you as a Home Pet Care pet sitter immediately. This is important if there is a change of pet sitters.

- Protects your clothing and coats from pet hair and dirt if the animal jumps up. I always want the pet sitter to feel comfortable picking up, petting and brushing the animals without fears about getting a good shirt, coat or pair of pants dirty or covered with pet hair. (It is also more socially acceptable to have pet hair on a work smock than on your own clothing!)

- It can be removed and your clothes underneath will still be clean if you have to stop anywhere to do errands between pet sitting calls.

- Customers like it. They have mentioned many times how professional it appears!

- It is FREE advertising! Keep them clean and pressed!

...I keep a small carpet sweeper in my car trunk and go over doorway and small area rugs with it on my last visit. Customers are impressed, "everything's just as I left it," they say!
Sharon Treweek

We keep dog bones in our car tied with our company color ribbon and a small slip of paper that says "Compliments of Pet's Best Friend," our logo and phone number. We give them to any dog owner we see. We recently left sheets with our clients asking for referrals (their friends). We sent a brochure to the friends saying that their friend used our service and wanted to share it with them. The referring client receives a discount on the next invoice. You hit your target market and have a testimonial at the same time!
Susan Baker, Pet's Best Friend Inc., Rocky Mount, NC

...I wear a "tool belt," but instead of tools it holds a small bottle of 409, a squirt gun, paper towels, pepper spray and other necessities. I never have to waste a second searching for something.
Jen Posner, Pet Pals, Greenville, SC

May/June 1997, Vol. IV, Issue 3

Ants are a problem in the summer, so put the pet's food dish in a shallow pan of water, such as a pie plate. Ants won't cross water to get to food - it works!
Candice Bishop, Homebuddies, Huntington Beach, CA

For dirty paws, I carry a spray bottle filled with water. Simply squirt on dirty feet to clean. This also works great on carpets. I never leave home without my spray water bottle! Also, I carry an electronic dictionary that fits easily into a pants pocket. It comes in handy for spelling on daily notes when it's been a long day and you're tired and "brain dead."
Sandy Naumchick, Bone-voyage Home Pet Care, Macedon, NY

Rub catnip on your shoes, hands, and lower pant legs to make instant friends with cats!
Patti Castleberry, No Place like Home, Carrollton, TX

Jan/Feb 1999 Vol. IV Issue 1

For "extra services" that you provide at an hourly rate, consider pricing these in increments of an hour. For example, if you typically charge $16.00 per hour for extras such as going to the store to purchase more pet food for customers, word it on your literature that you charge $4.00 for 15 minutes of personal services/shopping. This makes it more palatable and reasonable to customers.
Bryce Arnette, Georgia Network of Professional Pet Sitters

I ordered some pens with my business name/phone number, etc. I got tired of losing pens and not being able to find anything to write with at clients' houses. So, I like to leave the pen at the end of the sit. I also leave the pens at the grocery store, pharmacy, video rental store - everywhere I go. People actually do pick them up and call me. I also leave handfuls at vet offices and beauty salons.
Carol Rexer, Cat Care by Carole, Clear Lake, TX

To remove urine odor from carpeting: Clean the area by your preferred method. While area is still wet, place plain paper towels or a clean dry towel over the area and then place a cement block on top. The cement block will wick up the moisture and the odor into the towels and the block. It is really amazing how well this works.
Sharon Treweek , Home Pet Care, Montana/Colorado/Utah

March/April 1999, Vol. IV, Issue 2

A great way to get free advertising and do something good for our planet is to join the Adopt-A-Highway Program in your community. Here in Pennsylvania a 2-3 mile stretch of state road is maintained by civic

groups, businesses or individuals. The agreement requires maintenance approximately four times a year (only 3-4 hours each time), and in return, the state posts a sign with the business name at the end of each portion or road you have volunteered to clean.
Sharon Whitman, Brandywine Pet Pals, Chadds Ford, PA

Adopt-A-Highway Participants. L-R: Jennifer Armstrong, Sharon Whitman, Owner, Alex Irvine, Kathy Meitz and Anne Lenning, all of Brandywine Pet Pals.

Sept/Oct 1999 Vol VI, Issue 5

I've created a new service for my furry clients. During the summer, For Pets' Sake is offering field trips! We charge $17-20 for a round trip outing to a neighborhood park, to lunch breaks with the pets' owners, or even to PETSMART to pick out a toy of their choice. Oh, what fun it is to be a pet sitter!
Laura Michele Edwards, For Pets' Sake, Orlando, FL

I post pictures of clients' pets on your website so people keep coming back (to view it).
C. Lusk & N. Kushner, Tri-state Pet Care Plus, Huntington, WV

Lure cats out of hiding or down from trees by placing catnip out. Worked for me in 2 minutes max!
M. Leidlich, Kuddly Kritters, Miami, FL

July/Aug 1999, Vol. VI, Issue 4

For cats that won't take liquid medication, I put it on their back and they lick it off. For pills, I put them in sardines or tuna.
H. VanHeist, Mrs. Paws Pet, Sitting, Brighton, MA

May/June 1999, Vol. VI, Issue 3

I wanted to write and let you know the unique way Fur & Feathers celebrated NPPSW this year. I was able to obtain cooperation from a small local pet shop where I get a lot of my bird supplies to put up a box for a drawing. I created a decorated drawing box with an eye-catching sign, and informed my customers in my last newsletter that to celebrate NPPSW I was giving away a $50 gift certificate for in-home pet care. They could sign up any time in February with the drawing being held March 1st. In addition, of course, all the pet shop customers can sign up, becoming aware of my service. And, the big plus in this idea, I will use all the entries to send brochures to these pet owners. This is a win/win idea for the pet shop and me, and it is a relatively inexpensive way to advertise.
Sharon Gruenhagen, Fur & Feathers, Green Bay, WI

November 1994, Vol. 1, Issue 3

Ask clients the dates of their pets' birthdays and then surprise them with a birthday card on their "special" day. Clients will get a kick out of this remembrance, and it's sure to win brownie points for you!
Bill Foster, Paw Partners

If you don't keep a pet carrier in your car, you should always ask the customer where they keep one in the home. This is something that is never where you might think it should be, and in an emergency with a pet, you don't need to waste time having to locate the owner's carrier!
Eleanor Caldwell, Crazy 'Bout Critters

I stamp my Service Contracts and Telephone Reservation Contracts with "100% of gratuities go directly to your pet sitter." It seems to increase tips and my sitters love it!
Carol Proffitt, Pawprints Pet Care

August 1995, Vol. II, Issue 3

I had a bad experience when a client's refrigerator stopped running. They had two cats, and I didn't need to even open the refrigerator. I make it a point to check each client's refrigerator on each visit now!

I have invested in a Polaroid camera for my business. I take a Polaroid picture of each pet I sit for so that if one should become lost, I have a photo to show around. The Polaroid also helps to record damage at a client's home. You can use it to document existing damage (stained carpet, chewed table legs, etc.) prior to your pet-sitting assignment, or for insurance purposes to help your client should any damage occur during the sitting assignment (hurricane, earthquake, etc.).

The generic PSI Gift Certificates are wonderful! I'm using them at all the local vet clinics. Each time someone brings in their pet to be spayed/neutered, the vet's office will give them one of these gift certificates which I've stamped with my company name and written in "$5.00 off pet-sitting services."

President's Column
PPSW
Conventions
Pet Sitter of the Year
Miscellaneous

President's Column

In every issue of *The WORLD,* PSI Founder and President Patti Moran speaks to the members. With her roots deep in the pet-sitting industry, Patti has always been a hands-on leader. She is very involved with pet sitting and concerned about ensuring that PSI members are getting the very best of everything an association has to offer.

Patti's feelings for pet sitting and every single PSI member shine through in every one of the *WORLD* columns.

A Letter from the President

May/June 1999, Vol. IX, Issue 3

A few weeks ago, Dotty, and I had the pleasure of attending two network meetings. We first spent an inspiring afternoon with around fifty pet sitters in Towson, MD, as the Maryland Pet Sitters' Network convened for their annual meeting. So much good information was exchanged as we discussed Lyme disease, pet sitter safety, and shared business tips.

The next evening we spent with twenty-two attendees of the Northern Virginia (NOVA) Network who are supercharged about PSI's upcoming Take Your Dog to Work Day scheduled for June 25, 1999. It was invigorating to hear ideas exchanged about how this network plans to work together to make this event a success in their area.

It is so gratifying to see personally what happens when pet sitters come together for the purpose of networking. Especially when some of them admit they initially couldn't imagine how it would benefit them to meet and work with their "competitors!" If, at first, there is any hesitation or awkwardness on the part of attendees this seems to change as the meeting progresses and colleagues realize we are all caring professionals who are in this together. The mood softens, barriers come down, and constructive discussion and exchange begin. Before we know it, the hotel staff is there waiting to clear the room, or the clock is striking way past everyone's bedtime, and no one wants to leave! But depart you must, and as you drive away, you find yourself rejuvenated so impressed with your network members, and oh so glad that you came! You may even chide yourself a little for those earlier thoughts about your competitors... and, gosh, are you relieved to know someone now with whom you feel comfortable referring those reptile calls! Networking...why did I wait so long?

With 25 registered networks, I know that quite a few PSI members can identify with what I describe above. If you are not involved with a city/county, state or regional group of pet sitters, I encourage you to take "the plunge" and organize a network in your area. PSI can provide you with written materials as to how to begin the process. And, if a network is not available or feasible for you, don't forget that our annual Quest for Excellence Convention is the ultimate in networking--don't let it pass you by!

Burnout Alert

A topic that was discussed at both Network meetings was burnout. It seems this subject always rears its ugly head when two or more pet sitters start talking! Since it is an industry-wide problem, it is something that I can't forewarn pet sitters about enough. Networking can help in this area though. One, just having others to discuss it with provides some relief. Two, finding a colleague or two who are willing to "substitute sit" for you to allow a summer vacation or the time to attend your niece's graduation is a wonderful benefit of networking. Today's pet sitter is fortunate to have others to turn to through networks and associations to find solutions to common problems.

Since the busy summer months are at hand, I hope you will give serious consideration to what you need to do to make sure you stay in control of your business rather than letting it control you. Avoiding burnout often comes down to one little word, "no." No, I won't take new customers at the last minute... No, I will not accept assignments in neighborhoods where I am not comfortable... No, I will not provide late night visits... No, I will not cut my fees... No, I will not take a job in a home where the housekeeping is deplorable... and the list can go on and on.

Actually write these policies down and file them for future reference. Then, you can tell a caller with honesty and integrity that "the situation is not in keeping with your company's policies" as you say "no" to their business.

Instead, start saying, "Yes!" Yes to the continued enjoyment of your business. Yes to your rights and privileges as owner of your pet sitting service. Yes to time off for you, your family and friends. Remember the adage that success is often the journey, not the destination. Reclaim, own and live your journey as a professional pet sitter. And, have your best summer yet!

And now, read on,

Patti Moran, PSI President

Professional Pet Sitters Week is celebrated the first full week of March each year. It originated in 1995 as *National* Professional Pet Sitters Week, but the first word was later dropped to reflect PSI's worldwide membership numbers. PPSW is a time for PSI to salute its members, who have brought pet sitting to the forefront of the growing industry of home service providers. It's also a great time for pet sitting business owners to thank their staff pet sitters for their hard work and dedication during the previous year.

PSI and its members also use this time to promote pet sitting to pet owners everywhere as the best choice for at-home pet care. And, each year, PSI reminds its members that during PPSW they should take some time to do something special for themselves—after all, they are the most important people in *The WORLD of Professional Pet Sitting!*

Professional Pet Sitters Week

How Did You Celebrate PPSW '98? GREAT IDEAS TO CLONE FOR PPSW '99!!

Jan/Feb 1999, Vol. VI, Issue I

"I wanted to enclose my ad for the newspapers for Professional Pet Sitters Week. It was important to me not only to recognize my sitters, but also the pet-related organizations/vet/staff who have made our business, with their referrals, a success."
Alice Wilson of Williamsburg Pet & House Sitting, Williamsburg, VA

"Take all my sitters out to lunch and give them a pin from PSI. For clients, I hold Client Appreciation Week and offer one free visit—this week only. In the community, we put out donation boxes sponsoring the local humane society. We also wrote a letter to the Governor of Georgia for a PPSW Proclamation."
B. Fasnacht, Cumming, GA

"Acknowledge my staff by either sending a card to say 'Thanks for doing a great job', or take out an ad in the paper thanking them."
G. Zimmerman, Sinking Spring, PA

"Get acquainted with some other pet sitters in my area."
D. Star, San Antonia, TX

"I'm calling two radio stations to see if they will talk about it on the air. It's special!"
D. Fitch, Glen Arbor, MI

"Ten-percent of my total March profits will go to our local humane society. Also, I'll advertise in our local newspaper."
K. Deisenroth, Elkhart, IN

"Send out press releases and try to make customers aware."
J.Arbuthnot, Boutonville, AK

"Go out to lunch with another sitter."
J. Williams, Alpharetta, GA

"I'm forming a meeting with the other pet sitters in town, and hopefully we will continue doing this throughout the year."
C. Gossett, Evansville, IN

"Call other area pet sitters and wish them "Happy NPPSW!"
D. Warner, Portland, OR

"Host an appreciation breakfast for my sitters."
D. Olson, Littleton, CO

"My sitters and myself are attending a pet first aid course and going out for dinner afterwards."
D. Lyon, Allendale, NJ

The bank is handing out dog bones with my business cards tied to them. I'm giving 50% off first visit coupons."
C. Ersek, Glen Mills, PA

"Special ad in the local paper announcing NPPSW!"
P. Wooden, New Britain. CT

Beth Fasnacht of Pet Watch, Inc. in Cummings, GA, celebrated the week by taking *"...all the staff to lunch at a very nice restaurant. I gave Service Appreciation Certificates to all the sitters....I also put up a display at the biggest pet store in our area. We [also] offered one free visit during the week for our clients."*

Conventions

Pet Sitters International's

Quest

for Excellence

PSI's annual *Quest for Excellence* Convention began with a handful of pet sitters in Winston-Salem, NC. With each passing year, it has grown and improved and is now touted as the world's best source for networking and face-to-face educational opportunities for professional pet sitters.

The WORLD has brought news and information about every *Quest* convention to the entire membership— whether they were able to attend or not.

Pet Sitters International

1995 *Quest For Excellence*

Winston-Salem, North Carolina

I <u>HATE</u> Meetings…Why Attend a <u>Convention</u>?

by Mary Lou Bowie, Noah's Ark Pet Sitting Service, Troy, MO

March/April 1997, Vol. IV, Issue 2

Having worked for many years in the business world, I have attended my share of meetings, many of which could have been carried out in a telephone conversation. Why would a person like me fall in love with attending conventions?

The answer is simple: The conventions I am referring to pertain to a lifelong love of mine – animals – and to a whole new exciting profession for me – pet sitting. Combine those factors and the expertise of Pet Sitters International (PSI), and you are instantly involved <u>not</u> in a boring old meeting, but in an exciting educational concept called a convention – to be specific, the PSI *Quest for Excellence* Convention!

When I entered the world of pet sitting back in September 1994, I was really "wet behind the ears." My only assets were somewhat of a business oriented brain, an avid love for animals (having a household of cats myself) and knowledge obtained from reading Patti Moran's book, *Pet Sitting for Profit*. Pet sitting was an entirely new concept of pet care in my rural/ suburban area of Missouri. Shortly after opening my pet sitting business, *Noah's Ark Pet Sitting Service*, and joining PSI, I was delighted to learn of the upcoming first annual *Quest for Excellence* Conference to be held in Winston-Salem, North Carolina. I felt I needed to learn, learn, learn—and to meet and network with other pet sitters.

I attended that first annual PSI convention in October 1995 without knowing one other person. That lasted for about five minutes, as other pet sitters and I began to exchange information regarding locales, number of customers, types of pets we service and countless other ideas and stories. Aside from all the conversation and socializing at daily meals and the dinner/dance, PSI offered a wonderful range of classes presented by professionals in the fields of animal communication, legal and insurance issues, accounting, reptiles and birds. They also offered a special three-hour course on first aid and CPR for dogs and cats. One cannot expect to retain everything presented at those conventions, but there were handouts to keep on file, and I took voluminous pages of notes for future reference.

Having enjoyed the friendships made and knowledge gained at the first convention, I anxiously awaited the second annual *Quest for Excellence* convention, which was held in September 1996 in Williamsburg, Virginia. It was wonderful renewing pet sitting friendships and visiting with PSI staff. Seminars and workshops included care of exotic pets, animal nutrition, pet diseases, emergency/disaster planning, pet and house sitting, legal questions, writing newsletters and advertising. There was even a course on iguanas, which interested me, as I pet sit one. The course included several live iguanas.

I feel that if we are committed to being professional pet sitters, we need to be knowledgeable about the many facets of the profession and learn continually. That is exactly what takes place at these conventions when we listen and partake in the information presented by these professionals. I have also gained wonderful insights and ideas from just conversing with other pet sitters, as we all do things differently and have ideas unique to our particular businesses.

Aside from the brainpower absorption, business and conversations, the PSI conventions have many fun events for our pleasure. At the second annual convention in Williamsburg, there was a wonderful, "Ghosts of Williamsburg" candlelight walking tour. In addition, PSI had an expanded tradeshow with all kinds of pet sitting and pet-related items for sale. This gave every pet sitter a wonderful opportunity to talk to PSI staff members and to trade show vendors about their products and services. There was also a time when the Pet Sitter of the Year was honored and crowned, and, at this second convention, different businesses and pet sitters donated items which were auctioned off at a special auction, with proceeds going to an animal charity.

The convention hotels are also top-notch, with comfortable rooms, good eating facilities and easy access to the convention rooms and neighboring areas. The conventions are held in many different areas of the United States; of course, I am plugging for a St. Louis as a future site. I have made wonderful friendships. I feel a close relationship with the PSI staff, and everything I learn and gain at these conventions is a definite beneficial enrichment to my particular pet-sitting business. We are each unique within ourselves and with our own pet-sitting businesses, but there is so much presented at these conventions that will touch each of us personally and businesswise.

Several months prior to attending the convention, when all the reservations are made and dates confirmed, I send my customers a spring/summer newsletter giving them the exact dates that I will be out of town and explaining where I will be going. Several customers have asked if they will be notified again this year of my convention dates so that they can plan their calendars accordingly. One new customer asked me to be certain they were included in this pre-convention newsletter so that they will not schedule anything while their pet sitter is out of town!

I once heard someone say, about privately owned businesses, "If you want people to take your business seriously, you have to be serious about your business," and that is so true. All of my customers think it is wonderful that I attend these conventions and take the pet sitting profession so seriously. As a follow-up to attending each convention, I wrote a news article and submitted it with a picture to our local county newspaper. This costs nothing and is a wonderful advertising medium. In fact, every time I have done one of these articles, I have received inquiries from pet owners and have secured new customers for my business. In addition, at Christmastime, I send all of my customers an annual holiday newsletter and enclose a copy of the convention newspaper article. As mentioned above, my customers are very impressed with the fact that I attend these conventions, which enhance my knowledge and, in turn, affect their pets when they are in my care as their professional pet sitter.

I still hate meetings, but I love the PSI conventions, and I encourage all pet sitters to make their top priority attending the **next** PSI *Quest for Excellence* It will be three of the most worthwhile days you'll ever spend!

Pet Sitter of the Year

PSI Pet Sitter of the Year—It's pet sitting's highest honor. This is a special competition because nominations for the award come from the most important people in a pet sitter's life—their clients. It is the only award of its kind where pet owners play the major role in recognizing and honoring their pet sitters. And *The WORLD* introduces these extraordinary pet sitters to their colleagues.

It is an honor for a pet sitter to be nominated because the Pet Sitter of the Year sets a standard for other sitters and recognizes the winner for a job well done. The winner of the Pet Sitter of the Year honor is officially crowned during PSI's annual convention. The winner receives a wonderful assortment of prizes including a trip to the convention, a cash award and plenty of media recognition and publicity as the true royalty of the pet sitting industry!

1999 Pet Sitter of the Year™

by Patti Moran

March/April 1999, Vol. VI, Issue 2

The winner of the most prestigious award in professional pet sitting will have already been announced by the time you receive this issue, due to the editorial calendar we follow. Although you should already know who is this year's Pet Sitter of the Year, here is what you don't know:

- There was a great amount of participation in our 1999 Award. 541 nomination forms were submitted for 97 pet sitters as of the 1/15/99 deadline. More arrived after the deadline, but they were not eligible for consideration.
- Some clients submitted, literally, volumes about their pet sitter. The time and effort expended on your behalf was most impressive.
- What tired eyes the PSI staff has after reviewing 541 nomination forms! (We apologize upfront for any typos in this edition that our weary eyes may have missed.) While we do not have to read the nomination forms, since the judging is done by a veterinary staff, we just like to read "good stuff".
- How dear and valuable you are to your customers! They do recognize and appreciate how hardworking, conscientious, and caring you are! Many of you "walk on water" as far as they are concerned.
- That many of your clients actually called the PSI office "just to make sure" their nomination forms had been received and were eligible for consideration. They want to see your excellent work acknowledged!
- The numerous excuses we heard from clients who "meant to get it in by 1/15/99 but "the cat ate it" or "grandma died" or something equally suspicious prevented their making the deadline...And, no, bribes don't work!
- The great amount of thought and debate that goes into selecting the winner of this award. Dr. Lynn Roberts (our "Ask the Vet" columnist) says it gets harder each year to pick only one winner as so many pet sitters are so deserving.
- How proud we are at PSI as we read these glowing forms about the professionals we're fortunate to work with. Thank you for making PSI and the pet sitting industry look so good!

Something else you do know is that the Pet Sitter of the Year Award exemplifies the PSI Recommended Quality Standards for Excellence in Pet Sitting. And, you know that next year could find YOU wearing "the crown." And I hope you know that as a PSI member, you're in the best of company. If you don't believe me, we have over 541 nomination forms that attest to this fact!

Carol Proffitt, 1995 Pet Sitter of the Year

May 1995, Vol. II, Issue 2

Carol Proffitt of PawPrints Pet Care Corp. USA Inc. in Knoxville, TN, has been named the first recipient of Pet Sitters International's annual Pet Sitter of the Year Award. The award was established by PSI to recognize the contributions of professional pet sitters.

As Pet Sitter of the Year, Proffitt will receive more than $2,000 in prize awards and international recognition through the publicity efforts of the association. Her prize package includes two round trip airline tickets good for travel in the United States from USAir, a year's supply of IAMS pet food, two polo shirts from the IAMS company, complimentary lodging and registration at the 1995 *Quest for Excellence* Convention and gift certificates from R.C. Steele's pet products catalog and Patti Moran's Products for Professional Pet Sitters. A commemorative plaque will be presented to Proffitt denoting this achievement, and she will be formally introduced at the convention, to be held in Winston-Salem, NC, October 15-17.

Proffitt was selected to receive this year's national award from among 23 professional pet sitters who were nominated from 14 states. Judging was conducted by the veterinary staff of the Pilot Mountain Animal Hospital in Pilot Mountain, NC. The selection criteria was based upon responsiveness to the needs of clients, willingness to go above and beyond the call of duty, the quality of care provided to clients' pets, and human and animal customer satisfaction. Nominations of pet sitters deserving of this prestigious award were submitted in writing to Pet Sitters International. Nominations were accepted from clients, as well as colleagues of pet sitters throughout the United States.

Dr. Lynn Roberts, chairperson of the selection committee and author of the "Vets on Pets" column which appears regularly in the PSI newsletter, said, "We had our work cut out for us in making this important decision. What became very apparent to us in reviewing the nominations was the real winners are the pets out there who are fortunate enough to receive the excellent pet-sitting services these professionals provide."

Roberts also pointed out that several nominations for pet sitters were received from the "pets" themselves! "Reading these glowing testimonies from 'Rupert,' the pleased Dalmatian, and 'Boy,' the Maine coon cat who adoringly described his wonderful pet sitter, made the judging process fun," she said. "It demonstrates how fond these pet owners are of their pet sitters to take the time and trouble to 'help' their pets compose letters of recommendation!"

Proffitt, who describes herself as a lifelong pet lover, began her pet-sitting service in 1991. Pawprints Pet Care has a staff of 16 and provides at-home pet care to more than 1,800 pampered pets in the Knoxville, TN, area. When notified of her achievement as the first PSI Pet Sitter of the Year, Proffitt said, "I am so flattered and grateful to have been nominated by clients for this award. I have the greatest customers in the world-I even refer to our services as VIP pet care because we take care of very important people's pets. Pet sitting truly is the most satisfying career I've ever had!"

The Pet Sitter of the Year was announced in conjunction with National Professional Pet Sitters Week, March 6-10, 1995. The week-long observance recognizes the important contributions of professional pet sitters, many of whom spend 12 to 14 hours a day, seven days a week, 365 days a year providing at-home care for thousands of pets of all kinds.

Nomination forms for the 1996 Pet Sitter of the Year award will be mailed to all PSI members in the November issue. Nominations must be made in writing and postmarked by January 31, 1996, to be eligible for the '96 Aaward. Pet sitters may nominate a deserving colleague, and pet owners may nominate their pet sitter. For the '96 award, pet sitters may not nominate themselves.

Many clients may be interested in nominating a special pet sitter, so PSI members are encouraged to notify their customers of this annual award. Use your in-house newsletter or even just a personal note left for the client to read. Members may make copies of the nomination form for clients, or you can suggest that clients contact PSI to receive a nomination form.

This office has just learned that our '95 PSY winner is putting her USAir prize tickets to good use with a trip to California for some sightseeing and then continuing on with a cruise to Mexico! Carol, we hope you enjoy your trip and your reign as our first distinguished Pet Sitter of the Year!

The Year That Was:
Pet Sitter of the Year 1996,
Melanie Hocevar, Looks Back.

March/April 1997, Vol. IV, Issue 2

A telephone call from Patti Moran on a warm Wednesday in February in Phoenix brought the news that I had been selected as PSI's 1996 Pet Sitter of the Year.

Imagine my surprise when Patti actually crowned me with a lovely plastic, gold crown complete with Milk Bones, Meat Bones and Snausages hot glued all over it! I can't tell you how surprised Patti was when I told her I actually wanted to keep it! One of my good friends, C.R. Witkowski, owner of Puddies and Pooches, and a fellow PSI member could not attend the conference. When I arrived back in Phoenix, we arranged to go to lunch so I could fill her in on all that happened at the conference. Imagine her surprise when I entered the crowded restaurant with my crown on! We both had a good laugh, and it got lots of comments and strange looks from other guests in the restaurant!

I proudly display the crown above the credenza of my desk for all to see. Two of my cats have enjoyed the crown, too. They ate all the Snausages! To say the crown has been an enjoyment to myself, my friends and my cats would not be an understatement. Thank you, PSI.

I was excited, of course, but I had no idea what Pet Sitter of the Year would mean to me or my business. Boy, was I in for an exciting year, filled with numerous interviews for radio and printed press, not to mention the tremendous increase in business.

Initially, the increase in business was the first change I experienced. Upon making the front page of the local newspaper, I received more than 70 calls the same day. Some of the calls were from current clients congratulating me on the award. Many were from the local veterinarians asking me to stop by and reintroduce myself, but more

than three quarters were from prospective new customers. Since I am a small "one woman" operation, with a few ladies I can call on to give me relief, I was not prepared for the overwhelming response from the public. Suddenly, I went from 2-3 new customers per week to 10-12 new customers per week. I had to do some pretty creative scheduling to handle all the new business. I certainly did not want to let this windfall of business pass me by. I could never have purchased the amount of publicity I received both locally and nationally.

I was surprised at the number of calls I received from all over the United States from strangers who would read an article and call to congratulate me and ask for my help and advice in starting their own pet-sitting service. Both the telephone calls and the articles allowed me to put PSI in the spotlight and educate the public about what PSI is all about and how we, as professional pet sitters, operate. So many interviewers tried to make a joke out of the award and our professions. I diligently continued to promote pet sitting as a profession not to be taken lightly. I am pleased to say that I believe I did make headway in that area. The general public is not aware of what pet sitters do. My goal this past year was to educate each and every person that called on the following items:

- Credible pet sitters belong to PSI.
- We are professionals, doing this for a living.
- We are insured and bonded.
- We follow a strict code of ethics.
- We participate in continuing education.

Since I did not see the completed nomination forms from my clients, I had no idea what they said about me. I called PSI and asked them what made me stand out over and above the other nominees. I was told it was the answers to the question "Willingness of the pet sitter to go above and beyond the call of duty." As I told the attendees of the conference in Williamsburg, "I am sure I won because I have such well educated and articulate clients." Whatever they wrote certainly caught the attention of the judges!

I would be remiss if I did not include the most outrageous interview I did. It was with Bloomburg Financial Broadcasting which syndicates all over the US. The call came to me from their base in New York City. At first, the interviewer acted like the award was a big joke. I assured her that it was no joke, and that, although I did have fun in my job, it carried a lot of responsibility and should not be taken lightly. When the interview, which was being taped, concluded, I stayed on the line thinking that she was going to come back and wrap up the conversation. I think she thought she had disconnected the line with me. She started editing the tape and a fellow reporter walked by and asked what she was editing. She said, "Well, if you can believe this one, I just interviewed the Pet Sitter of the Year." The other reported said, "Cool! I bet that was lively and interesting!" She said, "All I want to know is, why I get to interview all the kooks?" Obviously, she did not know that I could hear everything they were saying. Her credibility went right down the tubes with me, as did that of the station.

Probably the funniest telephone call came to me at 5:30 a.m. the morning the announcement hit the wire service. A good friend and former co-worker back East was listening to the radio on her way to work and heard them announce that it was National Pet Sitters Week; they went on to name me as the 1996 Pet Sitter of the Year. She got so excited, and she was laughing and bouncing up and down in her car at the stoplight when she heard it. She looked over in the car next to her and saw an older man looking at her as if she were crazy. She got right on her car phone and called me. We had a good laugh, even though she had awakened me from a sound sleep!

One of the most noticeable changes after winning the award occurred in the attitude of the local veterinarians. Before the award, with so many sitter services in my area, the veterinarians really didn't give me the time of day. A few would recommend me, but once I printed the brochure announcing I was the recipient of the 1996 Pet Sitter of The Year, I suddenly gained credibility and received many referrals. Locally, that was probably the biggest change I noticed.

After 6-plus years of pet sitting, I was starting to burn out. I can tell you that this award certainly revived my positive attitude toward pet sitting. I can also tell you that I became much more organized and focused on what the award meant to me, my business and my future. I immediately set some goals I hoped to accomplish during the year and then set out to make them happen. I aimed for at least one written and one broadcast interview per month. I surpassed that goal. I spent a lot of time soul searching for a way to make the award "pay off." Both PSI and myself had hoped I would get some endorsement contracts from some of the sponsors of the contest. Although we worked that angle, none came my way. By the end of the year, I had to make a decision to either expand my service and hire more help or find another way to capitalize on the award. I am a true believer that no matter what the recognition is for (as long as it is positive!) that it is my duty to make it work for me as hard as I have worked for the award. Although I cannot at this time tell you what my plans are, if all goes according to plan, I will be expanding my service greatly in the Phoenix area in the near future. I would not have been able to accomplish this next plateau without PSI and 1996 Pet Sitter of the Year Award. To PSI, all of my wonderful clients who wrote such nice things and to the judges, I am truly honored that you chose me to represent you as PSI's 1996 Pet Sitter of the Year. Thank you and good luck to the 1997 award winner.

PSI Pet Sitters of the Year 1997! Helene & Sharon Jones Sisters Sitting Service, Ft. Lauderdale, FL

May/June1997 , Vol. IV, Issue 3

Sharon and Helene Jones are proof that the family that works together can become winners together. The sisters have been named Pet Sitter of the Year by PSI. The sisters, who operate *Sisters Sitting Service* in Ft. Lauderdale, FL, are the third recipients of the award. They reported that they were shocked and "extremely pleased" by their selection.

As it turned out, 46 of the sisters' clients nominated them, citing, among other things, the two women's charity work with seven animal foundations—most notably the Greyhound Rescue Society. "We thought we had the best customers in the world," Sharon said, "and now we are certain of it."

"Pet sitting is not just a job for us," Helene added. "It is our life. We play matchmakers and find homes for pets, and we tell everyone we meet to support animal causes."

Their own support for one such cause is impressive. "Actually, we would like to spend more time in animal rescue," Helene said, "but at certain times of the year our business is very demanding and we are unable to do as much as we like. We make rescues and education a part of our everyday living. We try to keep as active as possible in greyhound and Doberman rescue causes. When we take vacations (other than PSI conferences), we volunteer our time, money and energy in local or national rescue groups. We have also matched many stray pets with wonderful people."

The sisters went into the pet-sitting business together in 1983. "We were the first to begin such a business in our area," Helene explained. "At the time it was not really recognized as a business, but just a nice way to make a little extra money."

"We now have 300 to 400 clients," Sharon said. "Some call us many times during the year and others may call once a year. There are many that have been with us since we started."

Twice daily visits for people who are out of town and have dogs who need access to the outside is their most common service. They are also building up a large daily regular schedule for people who work and want to get their dogs out and exercised. They also provide overnight live-in service.

Until a few years ago, the sisters handled all the business themselves. More recently they have been using two part-time employees and have just hired a third to help with overnight service. "Our overnight or live-in service consists of staying in the home 12 to 14 hours, guaranteed," Sharon said. "We cannot stay there all day as we are very busy doing visits throughout the day."

Another change that they have made over the years is the narrowing of their target market. "When we first started, we would go as far as service would take us," said Helene. "Sometimes the travel was more time consuming than the visit itself. Now, we have cut our travel radius to approximately 15 miles."

As part of their honor, the sisters will receive more than $3,000 in prizes and awards, in addition to international recognition. This year's prize package will primarily be funded through The Iams Company, the new sponsor of the contest. Iams is furnishing a year's worth of pet food, Iams marketing apparel and a check for $500. Among the other prizes is a $100 gift certificate from Weaver Leather, makers of collars, harnesses and leashes. Prizes will also be given by Pet Products of Los Angeles, The Sherpa Pet Trading Company of New York and Pretty Bird International Inc. The sisters will also receive a free lifetime membership to PSI.

The Jones sisters will be formally introduced at the September *Quest for Excellence* Conference in Las Vegas, NV.

PSI received 500 nominations from 30 states. Judging was done by the Pilot Mountain Animal Hospital in Pilot Mountain, NC. Award criteria included the sitters' responsiveness to the needs of clients, willingness to go above and beyond the call of duty, quality of care provided to clients' pets and contributions to animal welfare.

Lynn Roberts, DVM, chairperson of the selection committee commented, "This year we saw an unbelievable degree of quality in the nominations. The extra effort that these pet sitters put forward in donating time, energy and even money to animal causes is just great!"

Roberts added that the judges' decision was a difficult one. "Many pet owners referred to their pet sitters as personal advisors," she said, "while some sincerely wrote that if their pet sitters quit, the pet owners could not go anywhere."

The sisters agree that of all of the changes in the pet-sitting business and in their enterprise, the organization of Pet Sitters International has had one of the strongest impacts on the industry as a whole. For the sisters, being named PSI Pet Sitter of the Year is a major career milestone.

"I was absolutely shocked and stunned," Helen said. "We knew our clients appreciated us, but it was a thrill to find out just how much!"

"I wasn't," said Sharon. "I thought we had a good chance of winning. See, we don't agree on **everything**!"

The Paragon of Pet Sitters
A Great '98 for Pet Sitter of the Year

by Susan Baker

March/April 1999, Vol. IV, Issue 2

It was a typical February morning at the office of Pet's Best Friend - answering the phone, taking reservations, typing the spring newsletter, burning a ham on the stove downstairs, setting off the fire alarm, calling the fire department to apologize for my stupidity, etc., etc., etc. Totally disgusted with my inability to do 5,000 things simultaneously and my burned dinner, I came back upstairs to my office to resume work on my newsletter.

At 10:05 a.m. the phone rang. I answered and forced a cheery business greeting (still upset with my ham cremation). "Susan, this is Cathy Jones with Pet Sitters International. How does Pet Sitter of the Year sound to you?" Honestly, I have no idea what my response was! I do remember telling Cathy that I would have to call her back to discuss details because I had to tell my husband, Van, and my best friend/employee, Lydia. I was so excited and in such a hurry to spread my good news, I may have actually hung up in Cathy's face! To say I was excited is a huge understatement. I'm not sure that Roget even has a word in his thesaurus to describe my emotions. I had no idea what obtaining the most prestigious and coveted title in the pet sitting industry was going to mean to me and my business in the year that followed.

The news spread rapidly and congratulatory calls started coming in almost immediately. Lydia told each caller that she was "trying to scrape me off the ceiling"...truth is, she's still trying! One client who had always referred to me as Sergeant Baker, because I run such a strict business, called to say that he had promoted me to General Baker because of the award. My pastor called posing as a potential client, "I'm looking for the best pet sitter in the world!" He announced the award in church the following Sunday. (His call will always be very dear to me since he was battling cancer at the time and lost his fight just eight months later at the age of 43.) My Bible study class held a party in my honor. A member of my Sunday School class placed one of my articles on the bulletin board in our class for all to see. My fellow church members—some of whom I didn't even know —greeted me in the lobby with congratulations.

I received hundreds of e-mails from clients, fellow pet sitters, cybersitters and potential pet sitters—so many that I had to raise my monthly AOL minutes to accommodate my responses and my budget! I also had to develop a form letter to attach to my e-mails for potential clients. I am still receiving e-mails from pet lovers who want to join our industry! One even sent me a cheesecake for helping her! One of my clients e-mailed me a scan of a picture of me and my pups that appeared in a newspaper. Van transformed it into wallpaper on my computer monitor. Another client added a link to my article on the PSI Web page to her own Web page! Letters and cards poured in. My first grade teacher (Yes, she's still alive, I'm only 40!) left a copy of the local newspaper article with a note in my mailbox saying how proud she was of me.

The following week we held our first annual dinner to honor our clients who called on us the most in the previous year. Lydia presented the opening remarks and then introduced me to our guests as the 1998 Pet Sitter of the Year. I received a standing ovation and a huge congratulatory welcome. I was so emotional that I could hardly give my speech. Keep in mind that this dinner was to honor our CLIENTS, but being the extraordinarily wonderful group that they are, they turned the whole event around and honored me instead. Kim Weatherly provided musical entertainment for the event and dedicated a series of songs to me including "Somewhere Over The Rainbow," "Hero," and "Wind Beneath My Wings." This was extremely special to me because Kim is the founder of Pet's Best Friend, so she knows firsthand the difficulties of being taken seriously and succeeding in a relatively new industry. (She sold the business to me five years ago and pursued a singing career.)

I even had a confrontation with the paparazzi! The morning after Cathy's call, I was pulling out of a client's driveway and Lydia was waiting for me in her car, camera in hand, hiding behind the hedges! Snap, snap, snap - a star is born! Lydia also had a tree planted in honor of my success in Virginia as part of the state's conservation project.

Lydia and I appeared on two local TV shows - one was a business interview show and the other a cooking show. The host of the interview show was already a client, and we picked up the hostess of the cooking show after the taping! We had to prepare two dishes for her show. (I found it to be somewhat hilarious and paradoxical to ask a pet sitter to cook on TV - do pet sitters actually have time to cook?) Both of our recipes came from PSI's *Eats 'N Treats* cookbook which we promoted on the show. We also presented an autographed copy of the book to our hostess. We appeared on the Fox 22 *10 O'clock News* with our clients' pets doing what we love most. Rusty the cat was the star. Rusty has gone to kitty heaven now, making this footage priceless to us and his owners.

I did 14 radio interviews with stations across the United States and Canada. A blurb about my PSY status appeared in Morning Mouth Magazine under Phoners (a list of ideas for radio station phone interviews), and also on the Wireless Flash News Service. All of the DJ's were very professional and, unbelievably, no jokes were made about our profession. I hope that some of these interviews benefited other PSI members in the various cities where the interviews were aired. I am still getting new clients, almost a year later, who say they heard about us on the radio or TV.

Printed media abounded as well. I am aware of four different newspapers that featured my story—two local, one in the PSI area and one in Los Angeles. Magazine articles appeared in both *Cat Fancy* and *The Pet Tribune.* Our Chamber of Commerce newsletter and my college alumni magazine ran articles with pictures. I contacted many other media sources  including magazines, TV shows, newspapers, and radio stations in an effort to educate the public about our industry, but was either turned down or received no response. The TV show *America's Greatest Pets* did interview me, however, I have not heard back from them as of this writing. I was amazed at how many clients, existing and new, called and said that a relative had seen my story in a publication out of town or out of state. It is hard to quantify the results of all the media attention we received because it is a continual process.

The corporate sponsors of the Pet Sitter of the Year Award were generous with their prizes. The IAMS Company provided me with a year's supply of dog food. PetLife Magazine gave me a cash gift and a year's subscription to their publication. Patti Moran's Products furnished a gift certificate. PSI awarded me with a lifetime membership to their organization, a gorgeous plaque, and of course, my 14 karat gold plastic, dog and cat treat studded crown. I displayed my crown at our Chamber's Business Expo in October —what an attention getter and conversation piece! Unfortunately, I cannot display it in my office. My four-legged connoisseurs don't view it to be quite the status symbol that I do! My gratitude goes to PSI and all of the corporate sponsors for their generosity and support!

Winning the PSY status enabled me to win another very coveted and prestigious award locally in June. Our Chamber of Commerce voted me the 1998 Small Business Woman of the Year. What a rush! To be recognized by someone in a field other than pet sitting - maybe someone IS finally taking us seriously! The Vice Chairman of the Chamber presented the award to me at the banquet; he is a long time client and said in his presentation, "She's been to our house a hundred times!" To be considered for this award, you must be an entrepreneur who is tops in your field. Now, I wonder where they got the idea that I was tops! Thanks again PSI!

In an industry that experiences tremendous owner burnout, the Pet Sitter of the Year Award definitely provides rejuvenation for its recipients! And then, to be able to win a second award because of your PSY status... WOW! Because of the recognition that I have received, my business has experienced significant growth, and I have had to add additional sitters to my staff. We are currently in the process of starting a second branch of Pet's Best Friend in a city about eighteen miles away. All of my success belongs to One much higher than me, and I give Him all the glory, honor, and praise for my accomplishments. I am sincerely grateful for the strength, endurance, and wisdom that the Lord gives me daily to persevere. There are very few people who truly enjoy their jobs and even less that succeed. My thanks to the PSI staff, the corporate sponsors, and the judges for making the Pet Sitter of the Year award possible.

Pet's Best Friend's clients are the best - just the fact that they took time out of their busy schedules to nominate us made us all winners. We take our work very seriously and feel that the bond and respect that we have with our customers is earned through our dependability, consistency, and true love for all animals. I appreciate our clients for the opportunity they have given us and for allowing their best friends to become our best friends.

A huge thanks goes to my husband Van and my dedicated staff for their endless efforts to provide the best in-home pet care possible! I also thank my own precious pets Bandit, Blaze, and Chester who continue to be my inspirations. My sincere appreciation to Kim for starting Pet's Best Friend. My only regret is that I didn't think of the idea myself.

It takes hard work and commitment to run a successful pet sitting business and each of you should be proud of what you do and your own accomplishments. Your clients DO appreciate you and the care you give their pets, so don't hesitate to spread the word about the Pet Sitter of the Year Award. Send out those nomination forms in your newsletters, leave them with your invoices - remember, if only one client nominates you, you're a winner. Take it from me, a pet sitter who has heard everything from "You do what?" to "I thought you just put a dog in the back yard and throw it a bone," to "What are you doing with your math and business majors, counting fleas!", the recognition is well worth it. You could be the next paragon of pet sitters. Good luck to the 1999 winner and all of my PSY successors!

1999 Pet Sitter of the Year: Heidi Kistler

by Janet Lee

May/June 1999, Vol. IV, Issue 3

Dedicated. . . professional. . . considerate. . . generous. . . responsive. These are just a few of the adjectives that dotted the pages of nominations for Heidi Kistler, owner of Pawsitively Pampered Pet in Oakland, CA, who has been selected as the l999 Pet Sitter of the Year. This national honor is considered to be the highest acknowledgement of pet care providers within the pet sitting industry. Heidi received a total of 54 nominations from her clients, employees and colleagues.

"Heidi is a million steps beyond your average pet sitter," client Susannah Breslin raves. "Her dedication, warmth, commitment and generosity are an ideal example for all other pet sitters. I can't think of a person more appropriate to represent the pet sitting industry on a national level." Clients Daphne and Dennis state, "We feel very confident when we leave our house and pets in Heidi's care. We know she is responsible and will use her common sense if any problems arise."

Jeremy Rexinger, who periodically works as an independent contractor for Heidi, says, "Heidi's first concern is always the pet!" And one of Heidi's pet sitting colleagues writes, "Heidi always strives to make pet sitting about more than just 'walking a dog'. I am truly amazed at the rate of success she has achieved in such a short amount of time."

Heidi, who started her business just over two years ago, exclaimed, "I have the greatest job in the world! I get unconditional love from the pets I care for every day." Elated at winning this prestigious award, she remarked, "I know how hard pet sitters work and I think we all deserve this award. I also want to thank PSI for the award, which gives credibility and visibility to all of us pet sitters!"

As 1999 Pet Sitter of the Year, Heidi will receive a lifetime membership to PSI, as well as free registration and round-trip air fare to the l999 Quest for Excellence Convention in New Orleans (Sept. 9-12), where she will be honored by her peers. She will also receive $500 from the IAMS Company, who has been a sponsor of Pet Sitter of the Year since1995. Heidi says she is looking forward to attending the convention in September and would appreciate the opportunity to endorse pet care products she supports. Fox News and local media in the San Francisco Bay Area have contacted Heidi to arrange a series of interviews in the near future.

Heidi is an avid supporter of the Friends of Oakdale Shelter (F. O. T .O. S). She says, "I am working to develop community awareness because I believe F. O. T .O. S. is helping our beloved animal friends have a better life." Heidi is trained in pet first aid and is currently studying various alternative health practices for animals, such as touch therapy. She also supports Kids Care Inc., a Texas organization that aids underprivileged children. Within the pet sitting industry, Heidi has assisted in the development of The East Bay Pet Sitter's Network, a group of local pet sitters who meet monthly. In March of 1998, she successfully completed a 25 hour self-defense course, along with several other pet sitters, to help foster awareness and confidence while pet sitting. She participates in  a newsletter network with other PSI members. By way of her own first-rate newsletter, The Pampered Pet Gazette, she passes on pertinent information to her clients and encourages them to respond both locally and nationally to the needs of animals.

Heidi graduated from U.C. Santa Barbara in 1995 with a B.A. in Cultural Anthropology. Her major allowed her to take a wide variety of classes, and she received a diversified education. She knew she wanted to start her own business but hadn't decided on a vocation. The idea of pet sitting was conceived during a brain-storming session with a friend. The Pawsitively Pampered Pet was born on March 1, 1997. She began by caring for the pets of family and friends and quickly built her business through word- of-mouth referrals. Her first year in business she worked 365 days without a day off! She now has a client base of approximately 300 and has anywhere from three to six independent contractors helping her out during busy periods. The services she offers include daily drop-bys, overnights and midday dog walks.

Heidi resides in the Montclair district of the Oakland Hills area with her three male dogs, Nalu, Buster and Smokey, and her three female cats, Thistle, Mopsey and Spike. With what little free time she has, she likes to go hiking on the coast with her boyfriend, Ryan, and enjoys cross-country skiing in the mountains of Northern California.

Heidi has many exciting plans for the future. She would love to swim with the dolphins in the Bahamas. She believes dolphins radiate a powerful healing energy and would be thrilled to experience their mystical aura first hand. In addition, Heidi wants to find time to volunteer at Best Friends Animal Sanctuary in Utah. Best Friends is the largest animal sanctuary in the United States, and it invites the public to visit and assist in caring for the many animals living there. Heidi hopes that by volunteering at the sanctuary during her reign as Pet Sitter of the Year, she can help promote awareness of the needs of abandoned animals. Her goal is to encourage the public to strive for the high quality of care she practices with her clients' pets and to donate their own time and resources to the various animal causes she supports. Heidi adheres to this quote from Ghandi: "The greatness of a nation and its moral progress can be judged by the way its animals are treated."

About the Author: Janet Lee is a friend and pet sitting colleague of Heidi's. She owns Friendly Care Pet Sitting Service and also resides in Oakland, California.

Miscellaneous

When a publication covers as much subject matter as *The WORLD*, there's bound to be some content that just can't be put in a specific category. This final section of *The Best of Our WORLD* contains some gems that are well worth sharing, but didn't fit into any of the previous sections.

Cartoon Reprint

Copyright MARMADUKE. Reprinted with permission of UFS, Inc.

May 1994, Vol. 1, Issue 1

"Marmaduke! Just because she's a dog sitter doesn't mean you sit on her!"

Our Clients are the Best

May 1995, Vol. II, Issue 2

Here are some neat, unusual or generous gifts from clients received by PSI members:

- One customer made homemade oyster stew and left me a note saying to take it home and enjoy it. Since it was Christmas Eve, I knew I wouldn't have a break in my pet sitting to make dinner. What a thoughtful gesture!

- A top and pants outfit from Lands End. The gift card was marked "From Chewie, to his other mother."

- On Valentine's Day, two Siamese cats that I sit for left me a beautifully wrapped bag from Evelyn and Crabtree. In it was a bath sponge, avocado oil, foaming bath gel and all natural Peter Rabbit Carrot Biscuits. And they say pet sitters don't have it good!

- A waterproof backpack for supplies to be brought on visits. (Her dogs lifted their legs on my old one!)

Coming Soon!

The Best of *Our* WORLD
Vol. 2 • 1999-2004